My Little Brother

A CHILDHOOD MEMOIR

Maiko Serizawa

Edited by D'Ann Mateer and Elisabeth Adams

ISBN: 978-1-77828-293-5 (Paperback)
ISBN: 978-1-77828-294-2 (Hardcover)
ISBN: 978-1-77828-292-8 (Ebook)

Dedication

In the memory of my brother, our community of tiny half-dilapidated apartments, and all those who raised us with love.

Contents

Prologue

Open a map of Japan. Right at the centre of the Main Island – where the island makes a big curve – is Tokyo, the national capital region. From there, follow the Pacific coastline to the north: up, up, up, and you'll come upon a city called Sendai.

As someone who grew up in Sendai, I'm proud that, despite being a rural city, its name is recognized across the country. Perhaps it has something to do with the fact that Sendai has a population of over a million, or that the city is directly connected to Tokyo by a bullet train. Or maybe it's because Sendai appears on the daily weather forecast programs on the national television network.

But among all the things Sendai may be famous for, the community where I spent my early childhood isn't one of them. Though it is close to city centre, nobody outside seemed to know about it. It's probably because the community's lifestyle was far from luxurious – its six apartment blocks were old, and each apartment was tiny and dilapidated – and people normally didn't care to explore such a place.

In any case, the name of the community doesn't bear mentioning.

What does, however, bear mentioning is that in the spring of 1991, just as I turned one, my father got a job at a university, and my parents and I moved from Tokyo to Sendai, into one of those six apartment blocks.

Little did I know that this community was where my biggest childhood adventures would take place. Where I'd meet my first best friends and play on my first favourite tree. Where my family would welcome a new life and where I'd experience my first big loss.

Part I

Baby Brother

(June 1993 – March 1994)

Arrival

Early June. I'm sitting in the old bathtub of our tiny, half-dilapidated apartment. Standing by the sink, my mother has just finished washing herself. Now she stands to do a breathing exercise. These days, she doesn't come into the bathtub because her tummy is too big. Or at least, that's what I think.

My mother takes several deep breaths. Resting my head on my elbows, my gaze is fixed on her round tummy. The day is approaching. The new baby will be born, and I'll become a big sister.

One late afternoon, under the pouring rain, I stand in front of my apartment block with my father, watching my mother disappear into an orange cab. She's now heading to the hospital to give birth to the baby.

A sense of wonder fills my heart. Though I don't know exactly how tomorrow will be different from today, I know a huge thing is about to happen. My little sibling – he or she – will be here in now time, and I'll finally be able to hold the baby!

June 19th. The news of the successful delivery arrives in early evening. It's a baby boy, we're told. A big baby, weighing close to eight pounds.

My father and I and my maternal grandmother, who has just travelled from her house in the countryside, rush the hospital to see my mother and baby brother. Once we arrive, however, I notice something isn't right. My mother isn't holding any baby.

"Where is he?"

"In an incubator," says my mother. "He wasn't breathing well. So, they've put him in the incubator."

The three of us eagerly follow the hospital staff to the window looking into a room full of newborns in little glass boxes.

Which one is my brother?

It's not easy to spot him when I've never seen him before and all the babies look alike. But somebody tells me which glass box belongs to my brother: the one with the largest baby. After all, my brother wasn't born prematurely. His reason for being in the room is something else. My mother said he hadn't cried upon birth like a healthy baby should.

I wish I could go close to my brother, like when my friend's little sister was born. She was in her mother's arms, and my friends and I drew near and even touched her. But now? My brother is tucked away in a little box, with a glass window separating us.

The next day, I'm walking down the street outside my apartment block with my grandmother when my friends' mothers call out, "Was the baby born?"

"He was born," I reply, holding my grandmother's hand. "But he's not well."

I think of my baby brother in that glass box. The baby that didn't cry. I wonder how unwell he is. I'm eager for him to get better so that he can come home, and I can touch his face.

After days of waiting, my mother finally comes home, but without the baby. I'm told he's gone through something called a surgery because there was a problem with his heart.

"The surgery was successful," says my mother. "But your brother must stay in the ICU for some time."

"ICU?"

As my mother explains it to me, a picture forms in my mind. In my imagination, the ICU is a bright red room. Doctors and nurses are bustling around, and there in the corner is that tiny glass box holding my brother.

My parents tell me I need to wait before I can meet my little brother. And that they'll make new arrangements for me while he's in the ICU.

Whatever it is, I'm ready. No whining anymore. Because now I'm a big sister, who is patient and helpful.

Blue Hydrangeas

Every night, after supper and bath time, my mother goes to visit my brother at the hospital. Since my father hasn't come home from work, I go with her.

"Come, sweetie, we're leaving." My mother's tense voice comes from the living room. She's always stressed at this time of the day. "We must be on time!"

There's a red basket of toy fruits my father bought me at the hospital kiosk shortly after my brother was born. Each night after taking a bath, I collect the fruits into my green bag and hang it from my shoulder. Since I'm too young to be allowed in the ICU and must stay behind in the waiting room, my toys keep me busy while I'm alone.

The roads are deserted at night. We drive across the river, down and up a winding road by a tall, rocky wall, and under a traffic light that has only one red flashing light. In no time, we arrive at the gate of the hospital's parking lot. After parking the car, my mother and I walk to the hospital entrance hand in hand.

On the way, we pass a bush of blue hydrangeas. Even in the dark, their full blossoms shine brightly under the street lights.

Once inside the hospital, my mother leaves me in the waiting room before going to see my brother in the ICU. When it's all done, we walk back to the car, and the bush of blue hydrangeas once again greets us with its gorgeous blossoms.

Whenever we go to visit my brother, the first corridor we walk through is wide and lined with shops and restaurants designed for the patients, the hospital staff, and the visitors.

One day, while walking down the corridor with my mother, we pass a storefront with a shelf of stuffed animals. Being a fan of plush toys, I slow down to have a look. They're Disney characters. The small Mickey Mouse sitting on the top looks inviting.

"Sweetie, we're not buying anything today." My mother's voice is followed by a tug on my hand.

"I know," I reply. "Just looking!"

After that, every time I come to the hospital, I look forward to seeing my Mickey Mouse. Whenever we walk by the store, I slow down just a little to have a good look before my mother pulls my hand to move on.

One weekend, I visit the hospital with my father. As we walk down the wide corridor together, I linger in front of the shelf of Disney plush dolls to look at my Mickey Mouse.

"Do you want something?" my father asks, noticing my gaze.

"I don't want anything," I reply. "I'm just looking at something."

"If you want, I'll buy one for you," says my father, surprising me. I try to figure out if I've heard him right, but he's already walking toward the shelf. "Which one?"

"That one." I point to the Mickey Mouse sitting on the top shelf.

My father picks it up and takes it to the cashier. He then drops the doll into my hand. "Now, we must get going!"

We start to walk again, hand in hand, but now, my new Mickey Mouse rests in my other arm. I cannot believe it's mine now. I no longer need to wait for my visit to the hospital to meet him. This Mickey Mouse is *mine,* and he can always stay with me.

From that day on, the Mickey Mouse accompanies me on my hospital visits. Every night, after supper and bath, I collect my toy fruits in my green raincoat bag and grab my Mickey Mouse before leaving home with my mother.

As soon as my mother leaves the waiting room for the ICU, I sit my Mickey Mouse next to me on the bench and open my green raincoat bag to take out the toy fruits.

The waiting room is tiny, with two brown benches facing each other. I always sit on the same side. Sitting across from me on the other bench are two older girls. They look kind and speak to me with smiles, but I don't interact with strangers. After giving them a cautious look, I continue to play on my own.

One evening, as I take my toys from the bag as usual, my hand slips, and the light plastic fruits scatter all over the floor.

My fruits! I jump to the floor, crouching and reaching for my toys.

To my surprise, the two girls also bend over the floor, picking up my fruits that have flown under their bench. They smile and help me collect all the toy fruits back in my bag.

After the incident, the three of us start talking. Like older sisters, the girls play with me using my toys and Mickey Mouse. By the time my mother appears at the door to pick me up, the room is filled with our laughter. We're playing and talking as if we'd known each other for a long time.

Shortly after the night, the girls stop coming to the waiting room. My mother says their family member must have been released from the ICU. I never see them again.

Daycare

While my brother stays in the ICU, I go to a daycare. I'm told it's because my father has to go to work every day, while my mother works two days a week. On top of that, my mother needs to be available for any emergency call from the hospital.

At daycare, my teachers and friends are kind. I quickly get used to their presence and become close to one girl. She and I both love dolls, and every day, we each pick a doll and play together. After awhile, we realize we have the same favourite doll – a girl with soft hair whose eyelids close when we lay her down and open when we make her sit up.

My friend and I are in love with the doll and play with her day after day. But no matter how much I love the doll I cannot take her home with me. That starts bothering me.

One day, I mention my favourite doll to my mother when she picks me up.

"Mommy, you won't believe it. This doll is so special," I explain eagerly. "She can open and close her eyes just like us!"

My mother listens, but she doesn't offer to buy me one. After several more attempts, I finally reveal my wish. "I want to have a doll like her."

My mother tries to distract me, telling me to wait until Christmas. She'll buy me one then, she promises.

Usually, I'm fine with a deal like that. I'm a patient big girl, good at waiting. But today, when my mother turns down my wish, something snaps inside me. As we pass the post office just around the corner from our home, tears roll down my cheeks and I break into a sob. I feel my world has gone dark as night.

Then something happens. My mother says she'll buy me a doll like the one I've just described to her.

Ten minutes later, we're back in the car, heading to a shopping mall in the city centre. Since my mother must be at home for any emergency call from my brother's hospital, she tells me that the shopping will be very brief. This time, I have no complaints.

As soon as we reach the mall, we run into the store and dash to the children's toy section, to a shelf full of pretty dolls. I look for one that looks like the doll at my nursery. My mother helps me search.

A few minutes later, I pick up a doll with straight dark brown hair and a gentle face, a doll that somehow reminds me of the one at my nursery.

"Sweetie, how about this one?" My mother appears from the end of the aisle, holding a different doll in her hands. This doll has curly hair and a lively face. She even wears a summer hat on her head. Though she looks different from the one at the nursery, she's very attractive. The fact that my mother has picked her out for me makes the doll special, too.

For a second, I'm torn between the two. The clock is ticking.

"Which one?" prods my mother, standing next to me. "Decide quickly, sweetie!"

I cannot give up the idea of having a doll similar to my favourite one at daycare. I choose the one I'm holding, and my mother and I dash to the checkout counter.

In the days following our shopping, I often think about the doll with a summer hat that my mother picked out. She really had a lively face. And the summer hat was also nice. Though I'm happy with my new doll, part of me wonders what it would've been like to bring that one back home.

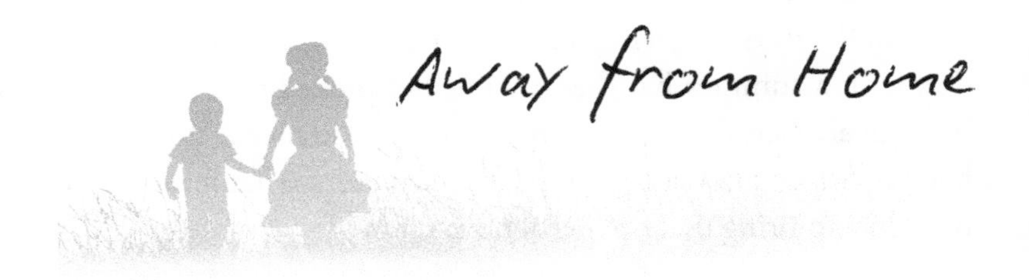

Away from Home

In August, my brother is transferred to the pediatric ward. Now that my mother has to stay with my brother at the hospital and my father has work every day, I'm sent to my maternal grandmother, to live with her for the month.

My grandmother lives with my uncle and his family in the countryside not too far from Tokyo. But because most of the family members are schoolteachers, it's usually just me and my grandmother at home from morning until my early bedtime in the evening.

Every morning, I wake up just after all the others have rushed off to work. My grandmother is in the kitchen with my breakfast ready on the table. After I finish eating, she goes out to tend her large vegetable garden, where she'll spend most of her day, and I go off to start my adventures. There's nobody to tell me what to do, so I can do whatever I want – as long as it's not dangerous, of course.

Unlike my family, my grandmother lives in a large house with a huge garden of both flowers and vegetables. The place is full of interesting places to explore. For example, there are several old shacks, two of which my grandmother uses for storage. When I go inside them, the dusty air tickles my nose. Both the floor and the walls are crowded with old and new farming tools and harvested vegetables. When I look closer, I find something else: children's ride-on cars, rusty and faded, which once belonged to my older cousins.

My grandmother comes inside to have lunch with me, then goes back to work again. Sometimes I join her in the vegetable garden out of curiosity, and she lets me pick tomatoes and other ripened vegetables. In late afternoon, she wraps up her farming work for the day to prepare dinner for the family.

In mid-August, the community's annual dance festival, *Bon Odori*, takes place in the city centre. My older cousin drives me to the festival with a few other relatives from the neighbourhood. Once we're there, we walk to the parking lot of the city hall. There are red lanterns hung everywhere, and in the middle of the parking lot is a tall pop-up tower where a woman is singing with drummers and flautists behind her. Many people, young and old, are dancing around the tower. I've never seen anything like this before.

Surrounding the dance floor are countless street vendors selling food and toys. One of the adults buys us a package of fried noodles. I don't think I've ever eaten such delicious noodles before, nor have I ever eaten food while standing in a parking lot.

From that day on, *Bon Odori* becomes my obsession.

One evening, after dinner, I ask my grandmother for scrap paper and a pair of scissors.

"Sure, but what are you going to use them for?"

"You'll see!" I answer breathlessly. "Something you'll like. I'll call you when it's ready!"

With that, I go to another room where I sit and craft several mock *gyoza* – Japanese-style grilled dumplings. I put them in a plastic container and secure it with an elastic band just like the food I saw at the festival.

When everything is ready, I run to call my grandmother. "Grandma, *Bon Odori* is starting now! Come quick, come quick!"

My grandmother stops what she's been doing in the kitchen and follows me to the other room.

In the centre of the room is a low table, and upon my signal, the two of us dance around it. My grandmother knows parts of the *Bon Odori* song, so she sings, and we dance to her singing. When the dance is over, I pick up the plastic container of pretend gyoza from the table.

"Since you danced so well, Grandma, you can have this food!"

"What a treat!" My grandmother never forgets to express her delight. "Oh, my, they look delicious, don't they?"

I go to bed, feeling happy and content that we've had such a wonderful festival evening.

In my grandmother's house, there's a room with a Buddhist altar where the spirits of my grandfather and other family members are celebrated and remembered. Before each meal, my grandmother brings the food to the altar, burns incense, and offers a prayer. I follow her and do everything she does right next to her.

The ceremony is long. I admire my grandmother's patience. My eyes remain wide open, closely observing her focused face as she murmurs the prayer. I have no idea what she's murmuring, but I understand this altar is a very special place for her.

During my daily exploration, I often make a visit to the altar, curious to know if there's anything other than my grandfather's picture that makes the place so special. I find some fresh fruits, a cup of green tea, a few small vases of flowers, and many decorations in gold related to Buddha and his life.

One of them is a small model of a sal tree made of some metal foil. It has several buds, some of them flowering, others not. It's a beautiful decoration, and I like the way the flowers look real.

The next morning, when I sit in front of the altar with my grandmother, I look for the sal tree again. The metal tree is in exactly the same spot as yesterday, but something is different. There now seem to be more blossoms on the tree.

The next day, I again observe the sal tree on the altar. *Yes, there are more flowers blossoming!* Excitement fills my heart. This sal tree not only looks real, it *is* real. The flowers bloom on the metal sal tree every day until finally there are no more buds.

It's around the *obon* season. Shortly after the sal tree fully blossoms, my grandmother and other family members bring it to the cemetery with other offerings, and there's no more sal tree on the altar.

My grandmother loves sparkling juice. Her favourite is the brand called Mitsuya cider. It comes in a tall, thin can with shiny green lettering.

Once the summer heat kicks in, she asks me, "Do you want sparkling juice?" When I answer yes, she walks down the corridor to her second fridge, and in front of my eager eyes, she pulls out the bottom drawer, a great portion of which is filled with cans of Mitsuya cider.

"Wow!" I cannot hide my amazement. I've never seen so many juice cans at once before. "You have so many, Grandma!"

"It's cold and delicious," she says as she picks out two cans from the drawer. Then we both head back to the kitchen where she takes down two glasses, one for me and one for herself. Back home, my mother wouldn't have trusted me with an entire juice can, but my grandmother is different.

She opens my can and pours some in my glass. Tiny bubbles shoot up from the bottom and the transparent juice sounds fizzy. I take my first sip. The moment the liquid hits my tongue, my eyes close at the strong sensation. "I love it!"

From that day on, this becomes our ritual. When we sit down for lunch, my grandmother asks, "Do you want sparkling juice?" And together we help ourselves to the cold, refreshing treat of Mitsuya cider.

One evening, a man visits from the newspaper company to collect the monthly subscription fee. I notice the visitor from the window while playing on my own, but being cautious around a stranger, I immediately call my grandmother.

My grandmother offers the guest a cup of green tea while they sit on the carpet next to the entrance. It's a custom that doesn't exist in my neighbourhood. Hiding behind a pillar nearby, I watch the conversation unfold between the two adults.

After chatting for some time, my grandmother hands money to the man from the newspaper company, and he, in turn, takes out a folded piece of cloth and opens it on the floor. Curious to see what's inside, I come out of my hiding place and sit next to my grandmother. There on the piece of cloth is a mountain of coins.

"Wow, is this money all yours?" I ask the newspaper man in awe.

He laughs but doesn't respond to my question.

"Why do you carry your money in a cloth?" As far as I know, money is always carried in a wallet, not in a cloth like this.

The newspaper man laughs again. He doesn't respond to this question either. He takes several coins from the collection and hands them to my grandmother. "Here's your change."

As soon as the newspaper man leaves, I ask my grandmother if she can give me some coins and a piece of cloth. She doesn't have as many coins as the newspaper man, but she gives me enough so that they make a jingling sound in my hand. For the cloth, she gives me a handkerchief.

With coins in the handkerchief, I go back to the entrance hall and sit down where the newspaper man sat a few moments ago. Then I open my handkerchief and shift around the coins, making a jingling sound, just like he did. A smile of satisfaction spreads on my face.

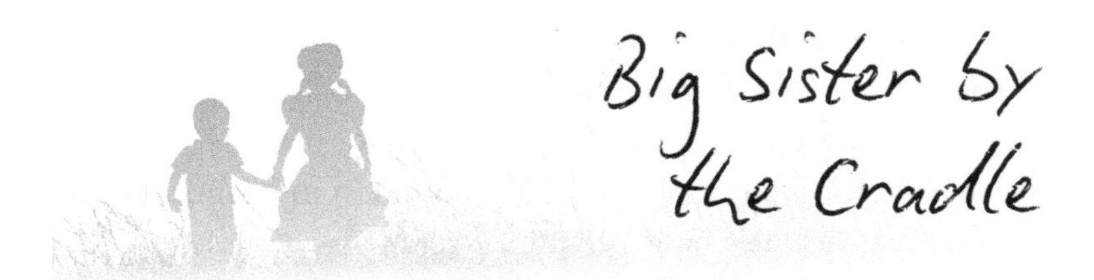

Big Sister by the Cradle

When I come home from my grandmother's house in late August, my little brother is at home. Finally, after so much waiting, I can hold him!

My baby brother lies in a tiny cradle on the floor. It's the same one I once used as a baby. I sit down next to the cradle and look inside. *This* is my brother that I've looked forward to meeting for so long, that I've already talked so much about wherever I went. Finally, he's here. And I am his big sister!

From that day on, I'm glued to the cradle. Whether he needs me or not, I'm always beside my new baby brother, talking to him, singing songs to him, reading stories to him, and gently swaying the cradle for him. I'm so happy having my baby brother that I cannot leave him alone.

On weekday evenings, after dinner, my mother runs warm water in the bathtub. My father hasn't come home yet, so it's just me, my mother and brother. As soon as the bathtub gets full, my mother ushers me to the tiny bathroom adjacent to our tiny kitchen.

Everything must be done quickly because my baby brother is with us. First, my mother places him in a safe spot outside the bathroom door and washes me. Once I'm in the bathtub, she quickly washes herself, and when she finishes washing, it's time for me to get out. My mother then picks up my baby brother to bathe him.

As soon as I change into my pajamas, I hurry to the living room, where I spread my father's big tatty brown bath towel on the carpet, making sure it's spread evenly. Once that's all done, I call out at my top voice, "It's ready, Mommy!"

Upon my signal, my mother shuffles out of the bathroom with my brother in her arms and joins me in the living room. I eagerly watch as my mother carefully lays my brother down on the towel. This is my favourite part – to see him happily stretch his arms and legs on the towel I've prepared.

"Thanks, sweetie," says my mother, and I grin.

This is our night routine.

My baby brother has heart disease.

This is a fact that never leaves my mind. Even though he's now with us at home, there's a constant reminder that my brother is different from a normal baby. Like the long trace of stitches that runs across the centre of his chest. Or the amount of milk he's allowed to take each day.

Because of his heart condition, my brother is only allowed to feed a small amount every day, which is never enough for a baby of his size. Every evening, my brother cries out of hunger, and that's when my mother takes both of us for a walk. She calls it our evening walk.

With my brother secured on my mother's back, the three of us walk out of our tiny apartment, into the fresh evening air of early autumn. The familiar path to the playground is empty. There's something exciting about being the only ones on the street. I skip and sing as I lead the way.

A few moments in, my own shadow on the street snags my attention. Above my head, shining bright in the sky, is a round full moon.

"Mommy, look!" I stop. "We're not alone. The moon is here, too!"

When I resume my walk, the moon follows me. I run, and the moon also seems to speed up. Suddenly, a sense of wonder fills my heart. "When I walk, it walks. When I stop, it stops, When I run, it also runs! Why does it do that?"

"I wonder why," says my mother from behind me. I don't hear my brother's cry anymore. "Maybe the moon wants to walk with you."

"Really?"

I start moving again. This time, I make it harder for the moon. I walk, stop, then run. I do it quickly. But the moon follows me without missing a beat. "The moon follows me!" I exclaim as I run. "The moon follows me!"

My brother is now all but quiet on my mother's back. Together, we continue our walk under the magic of the evening sky.

Group Photo

One day, there's a large gathering in our community of apartments. It's a farewell potluck party for my friend whose family is moving to Tokyo. Several mothers, boys and girls of my age, and our younger siblings come together in one of our small apartments with homemade meals and desserts.

I spend most of the time playing with the friend who's leaving. She and I put some funny masks on our faces. We giggle like mad people when adults call out and tell us it's time for a group photo.

In the largest room of the tiny apartment, all of us – both the children and the mothers – line up in rows. I sit in the front row next to my friend. We take a few photos, and while everybody gets ready for the next shot, I find a pair of toy sunglasses on the floor.

"What's this?" I pick them up and try them on. My friend laughs, and I grin back at her.

"Are you ready?" the person with the camera calls out. "One, two, three, say 'peace'!"

Everybody smiles at the camera.

"Who's that with the sunglasses?" a voice says. "Why don't you take them off? We can't see your face!"

"Don't worry!" I reply. "I like my sunglasses!"

The shutter is released one last time as I beam a smile under the black sunglasses.

Little Brother

Winter arrives, and I'm sitting on the floor of our tiny living room engaged in my favourite activity: playing house. Spread in front of me is a collection of small plates and cups. The imaginary feast is about to begin. With a huge smile, I turn to my guest – the first real guest I've ever had in my life.

My baby brother has little idea what's going on, but his gaze eagerly follows my movements. As soon as he learned to sit by himself, I invited him to play house with me. It doesn't matter that he cannot yet talk. I still want him to enjoy the imaginary meal I've prepared. Now, he sits next to me with his back propped against a pillow my mother placed for him.

Having a guest boosts my mood, making me the most caring host in the world. I describe the content of our feast, then scoop up some food from the plate with a spoon.

Since my brother is too small to eat by himself, I carry the imaginary food to his mouth, just like my mother does during our meal. My brother is a talented guest. As soon as I bring the spoon to him, he opens his mouth as if eating.

The imaginary feast lasts for quite some time, and my brother follows along without complaints. He looks happy. He responds to my talking with smiles and laughs, welcoming my attention.

One cold, overcast day, my mother takes me out to the local Shinto shrine for a festival. Both my father and brother are napping at home, but my mother decides to take me out for a quick visit so I can at least see the festival. We should be back soon, though, because when my baby brother wakes up, he'll cry for my mother.

It's raining outside. I'm wearing my green raincoat. After quickly finishing our greeting at the shrine, my mother and I walk down the stone steps, heading back to our car. Normally, we enjoy the festive atmosphere by browsing the many vendors along the passage, who are selling various kinds of food and toys. But today, we don't have time for that. We must get back home.

My eyes drift to different items displayed in front of each vendor. I know we must go home, but I feel sad about leaving without getting anything special, like cotton candy or a water balloon, something I can only get at a festival. Are we just going back home like this?

We pass another vendor. This one sells traditional lollipops. They are transparent and come in different shapes. Suddenly, my mother walks over to the vendor. She asks for a lollipop, and the vendor picks out a yellow one and hands it to me. The lollipop has the shape of a bird.

As I marvel at the beautiful candy in my hand, my mother grabs my other hand and starts to run. We run down the rest of the stone steps hand in hand, me in my green raincoat, holding the lollipop tightly. The shiny candy looks even more colourful against the gray sky and the wet stone steps underneath us.

One winter morning, my mother takes me and my brother to her workplace to make photocopies of her teaching materials. The copy room is empty and peaceful, the gentle sound of the heater echoing in the room. My mother makes us sit by the window while she uses the copy machine. My brother and I play quietly with our hands.

Suddenly, the door opens and one of my mother's colleagues comes in. They start chatting, and after a while, the lady walks over to us, comments how lovely we are, and gives us two little teddy bears – one brown and one white.

I immediately reach for the brown bear. In my head, a teddy bear is always brown, so the brown one is mine. But the moment I take the bear, my brother reaches over and snatches it away from me.

"You can take this white one," I say to him, gently replacing the brown bear with the white one. "Look, it's cute, isn't it?"

My brother, who usually goes along with whatever I suggest, isn't happy. He reaches for the brown bear again and takes it away from me. Now I'm upset.

"This one is mine!" My voice is raised. "You can take this white one!"

The brown bear travels between my hand and my brother's hand multiple times until our movements become aggressive and our voices escalate. Finally, my brother cries, grabbing my mother's and her colleague's attention.

"What's happening?" My mother comes over.

"I want this brown bear, but he takes it away from me," I explain, half-whining.

"You also want this one?" my mother asks my brother as she hands the brown bear to him. The moment the bear lands in his hand, my brother stops crying.

"Let him hold it until we go home," says my mother. "Why don't you take the other one?"

"But I don't like the white bear," I protest. "I like the brown one!"

Behind my mother, her colleague looks stunned. I wonder if she's feeling bad for not having brought two brown teddy bears.

"That's enough," snaps my mother, embarrassment and irritation visible on her face. "We're going home now."

She then turns to her colleague. "I'm so sorry – they sometimes fight over silly things."

"Oh, that's normal for siblings!" says the lady, smiling again. "They're truly lovely!"

The three of us leave the room in a hurry – my mother probably doesn't want us to continue the fight over the teddy bear in front of her colleague.

Once at home, I take the brown bear and hand the white one to my brother. This time, however, he loses interest in the teddy bears altogether and turns to his other toys. Because I still want the brown teddy bear, I keep it in my toy box.

Part 2

Family of Four

(April 1994 - March 1995)

A Delightful Disruption

One early summer morning, I play with my dolls in the back room of our apartment. On the other side of the room, in front of the wide-open window, is my mother doing her daily housecleaning. While vacuuming the floor, she's found a patch of mould on the wall, and now she's laser-focused as she scrubs the dark spots with a hard sponge.

My baby brother crawls around our tiny home as usual. He's just turned one. Since it's a warm day, my mother hasn't put a diaper on him out of concern that it might irritate his skin. He crawls and crawls, and after a while he stops next to our mother, curious to see what she's doing, but she's too focused on her task to notice.

After several attempts to catch her attention, my brother turns around and sits on the floor right in front of the window. He sits there for a while, keeping a straight posture, being unusually still.

How strange! I look at my brother carefully. *He never sits quietly like that!*

The next moment, my brother starts moving again, away from our mother.

But he left something on the floor.

As I watch closely, the thing on the floor becomes clear: a solid poop, shining in the sunlight coming in from the window.

"Mommy!" I shout. "Look what's behind you!"

That's when my mother finally turns around and finds my brother's piece of artwork.

"Sweetie! You pooped!?"

She jumps to her feet to grab my brother before there'll be more mess in the room.

I roll with laughter as my mother runs after my brother and then comes back to clean up the poop on the floor. What a wonderful disruption!

Family Trips

In the summer, my family goes on a road trip to a famous mountain area north of our town. When we come to a lookout with a fantastic view of the valley, my mother suggests we should take a picture there. She signals us to line up while adjusting her heavy black Pentax camera in her hands.

We stand on a cliff with a wooden fence behind us, one designed to prevent people from falling. Holding my baby brother in his arm, my father casually sits on the fence. As soon as I see them, I also want to sit on it. I try to climb, but the fence is too high for me.

"Sweetie, look here!" my mother calls out from behind the camera, but I'm busy trying to climb up next to my father and brother.

My father looks down and finds me struggling. "What are you doing?"

"I want to sit on the fence, too!" I cry.

Balancing my brother in one arm, he uses the other arm to pull me up.

Five seconds later, I'm sitting next to my father on the fence, smiling.

"Honey, watch out so that she won't fall!" my mother calls to my father.

"I know, I know, don't worry," replies my father.

Then the shutter is released.

There are two pictures of this scene. In one of them, I'm standing next to the fence, crying with my face up while my father looks in my direction with an expression that says "What's the matter?" In the other one, I'm sitting on the fence next to my father and brother, and everybody is smiling.

On the second day of the trip, we visit an old mining site in the area. My parents say that inside the former mining cave there's an interactive museum where we can learn about the history of the mine and the people who once worked there.

"A cave?" My eyes sparkle with excitement. "Are we going inside a cave?"

I've only read about caves in my story books, but they always sounded like a lot of fun – places for a real adventure.

"Oh, I can't wait to see the cave!" I jump up and down. "I can't wait to be inside the cave!"

As soon as we get to the museum, I shoot out of the car to the ticket office, and once we all have tickets, I start ahead of everybody into the mining cave.

There's a gift shop at the entrance, next to which stand three human-sized "dolls" dressed in work clothes. My merry mood vanishes. These three "men" look real. They're even nodding their heads like live humans. Eerie.

My parents catch up with me and ask, "Why aren't you walking, sweetie?"

Keeping my eyes on the fake men, answer, "I'm scared."

Both my parents laugh. "They're just dolls, saying hello to you!"

Suddenly becoming very cautious, I walk closely behind my parents. They're eager to learn about this mining cave, and my little brother, piggybacked on my father, seems totally unbothered. I don't understand how they can all remain so calm when there's a good chance that those three men will spring to life and start chasing us like ghosts.

As we move toward the first display of the museum, I find more "dolls" in the cave. In fact, they are part of the display, giving us visitors a better idea of how people used to work in the cave. Some are static, but others move when we press the explanation buttons.

"I'm scared, I'm scared!"

My fear of the "dolls" only grows bigger. As I follow my parents from one room to another, I try not to look at anything, and whenever my mother tries to press an explanation button, I scream.

"Don't press it, don't press it! They're going to move!"

Finally, my parents have had enough. My little brother is transferred to my mother's back, and I piggyback on my father. As soon as I settle on my father's back, I shut my eyes and ears. I don't want to see or hear anything in this eerie cave.

Some time passes. My mother taps my shoulder, telling me to open my eyes. When I refuse, she scolds me. "We're in the gift shop! There are no dolls anymore."

I slowly open my eyes. Yes, it's indeed a gift shop. We're out of the cave.

As we walk back to the car, my parents tell me how much I've missed.

"Even your little brother was having fun toward the end when he saw dinosaurs. But you didn't see anything!"

I don't see how dinosaurs can appear among those eerie human dolls, but maybe they were part of the decoration.

Whatever I missed, I cannot be happier to be back in my ordinary life, away from the cave, from the scary dolls.

Later in the summer, my family visits the zoo in our town.

My little brother rides in the stroller while we walk around the park. It's a very hot day, and after walking through a crowd of people for a while, I feel tired. Suddenly, I'm jealous of my brother. Why is he having such an easy time in the stroller while I have to walk? This is not fair! "Mommy, I also want to ride in the stroller."

Surprised by my sudden request, my mother thinks for a second. Then she says, "Sweetie, you're too big for the stroller, don't you think?"

"But my brother is always in the stroller," I whine. "I also want to try it!"

"There was a time," sighs my mother, "when we pushed you in the stroller, sweetie, but you don't remember it."

Seeing that I won't budge, my mother agrees to put me in the stroller. My brother is transferred to my father's arms, and I happily get inside the stroller.

But the excitement doesn't last for long. The stroller is indeed too small for me, and I don't feel comfortable. After a while, I call my mother, "I want to walk." I climb out of the tiny stroller without even waiting for her reply.

"Why? You don't like it?"

"The stroller isn't comfortable. I like walking!"

And so, as if I always preferred it, I march on my own two feet. Never again do I want to be pushed in a stroller.

Community of Tiny Half-Dilapidated Apartments

Inside our community of apartments, there are many old trees: rows of cherry blossoms in the back of my apartment block, a huge willow in the square playground in front of my apartment's balcony, and persimmon trees and Japanese plum trees on the other side of the community.

Of all the trees, there is one Japanese plum tree that my friends and I love. With its bottom branches stretching out low along the ground, the tree has a perfect shape for us to climb.

Except during winter, this Japanese plum tree is where my two best friends and I spend most of our time playing house together. Each of us chooses a branch for a private room, then another branch for our living room. My room is usually the thick, curved branch near the bottom, while my adventurous friend, Karen, takes the highest branch she can reach. Sakura usually chooses a branch in the middle. For the food, we pluck plums and serve them on leaves.

After setting up everything, I drift off to a daydream on my favourite bottom branch. Everything is peaceful here. As I listen to my friends' voices above me, I smile at the magic of our little paradise.

One afternoon, we're playing house in the Japanese plum tree as usual when suddenly, Karen climbs up the tree even higher. She goes up and up to a branch that's out of our reach.

"You're up too high!" I shout, unable to hide my fear. "What if you fall?"

But Karen seems unconcerned. She laughs. "It's really fun up here," she says, looking around. "You should also try it!"

Sakura refuses, saying the branch is too high for her. That somehow triggers me. "I can do that!" The bold words leave my lips before I can stop them. "It's not difficult at all! I can climb up high just like you!"

When Karen climbs down, I climb up. I go up and up, desperately wanting to sit on the branch my friend sat on earlier. In no time, I reach a spot where the branches become thinner above. I sit between two branches, and for the first time, I look down.

Suddenly, I realize how far up I've come. Two anxious faces are looking up at me. I try to move, but now my bottom is caught between the branches. I'm stuck.

"Aren't you coming down?" Sakura asks from below.

"I want to," I reply. "But I can't!"

"What do you mean?"

A sense of panic seizes my body, and tears well in my eyes. "Help!"

Upon my cry, my friends run to call a mother nearby who's been supervising us. She immediately comes to our tree and finds me stuck between two branches.

"Oh dear!" She smiles up at me. "You went up quite high! You couldn't climb down, hmm?"

The next second, she scoops me up from the tree and puts me down. Relieved to find my feet on the ground again, I promise myself I'll never, ever climb high up on the tree. I'll stick to my favourite thick, curved bottom branch.

On the back end of our community, not too far from our favourite Japanese plum tree, is an open space surrounded by thick, tall bushes where local bus drivers come to spend their time out of service. Today, I play house with Sakura, Karen, and Madoka, another close friend a year older than us, in one of the bushes.

With few people walking by, the place is the most hidden and adventurous among all our spots. Sometime in late afternoon, a distant sound of music reaches us from the university next door, providing a nice background to our imaginary family drama. My parents once told us it's a student brass band practicing.

The sun has just started setting on the horizon when Madoka suddenly trips on a rock and falls face down on the ground, breaking into tears. Though the only visible injury is a small cut on her knee, we all panic. Madoka rarely cries for small things.

"I'll call her mom," says Karen, quickly getting to her feet.

While we wait for rescue, Sakura and I try consoling Madoka by telling her funny stories. Little by little, she recovers from the shock and a smile comes back on her face. By the time her mother arrives, she's laughing with us.

"She fell and got hurt," we explain to Madoka's mother as soon as she sits down next to us. "Look!"

After a quick examination, she applies disinfectant on the cut on Madoka's knee, then covers it with a bandage. "It's all good," she says to us. "There's nothing to worry about." She then turns to Madoka. "You were crying, hon, weren't you?"

"But *how* do you know?" I exclaim, my eyes wide with surprise. Madoka stopped crying a while ago. She's laughing now.

"Well, I can see a trace of tears on your cheeks," she laughs as she points to Madoka's face.

"Oh!"

We all laugh, and after she leaves, the four of us go back to play our family drama for some more time before dusk. As we play, I keep thinking about what Madoka's mother said about the trace of tears.

Right in front of my apartment block is a square playground with a huge willow in the middle. Whenever my two best friends and I are not playing on the Japanese plum tree, we're found on this playground, playing on the slide or the basket swing, or picking flowers. We can easily spend the whole afternoon here, making up new stories and games, one after another.

One of my favourite things to play here is a game we invented called "Help Me!" This game is simple. First, we all sit at the top of the slide. Then, one of us falls on the slide backward, stretching out her arms and screaming "Help!" while the other two try to help her get back to the top.

In order to make the game interesting, though, the others not only help, they also create obstacles by stomping on the slide and making it shake. We picture ourselves on a clifftop, trying to save our mate from disaster.

Right at the centre of the metal floor at the top of the slide, there's a tiny hole I can poke my finger into. When I'm stationed there as part of the helper team, I sometimes look through the hole. I see nothing but the grassy ground several feet below. Yet seen through this tiny hole, it feels magical, making me believe that I'm hovering really high above the ground with my friends, having a real adventure.

After a while, my friends call me and I go back to participating in the "Help Me!" game with a loud scream and a renewed sense of excitement.

In July, a baby boy is born to Sakura's family. My friends and I all visit the hospital to meet the newborn, a tradition in our tight-knit community where we treat each other like family members.

My mother, little brother and I visit the hospital. We go there with Karen, her mother and little sister. Together, we march down the corridor to the room where Sakura's mother holds the newborn.

Once in the room, we circle her and the baby. "So tiny!" we children exclaim. "He's a baby boy!"

My one-year-old brother is quiet, his eager gaze fixed on the newborn. This is his first time to see any baby from so close.

Suddenly, Karen's little sister comes running with something in her hand – a tangerine. She holds it out, but her mother stops her. "Honey, where did you get that?"

Karen's sister is an energetic and affectionate child. I'm not surprised she's appeared with a tangerine. But her mother is upset. She insists on knowing where the fruit came from, and as soon as she learns it belongs on somebody's bedside table, she dashes to return the tangerine. The rest of us look at each other and burst into laughter.

Though the tangerine has returned to its owner, I don't forget that Karen's sister meant to make it a welcome gift to Sakura's baby brother.

Bath Time

On weekday nights, my mother, brother and I take a bath together. After washing, when we all sit in the bathtub, my mother and I both listen to my brother's breathing sound, which is a bit funny, like the air is bubbling inside him. On my brother's chest are stitches from his heart surgery. *He's different from me.* I listen and watch with a sense of wonder. *Because he has heart disease!*

I can't stare for too long, though, because my brother starts giggling under our quiet gaze.

On weekends, I take a bath with my father. He first washes me, and once I settle in the bathtub, I start playing with toys. Among my toys are several empty bottles of my brother's heart medication and a few plastic syringes.

While my father shampoos his hair in the washing area, I reach over to the white bubbles foaming on his head.

"Excuse me, Daddy." I scoop up some bubbles in an empty medication bottle. "I'm making a special potion that can cure any disease in the world!"

I mix the white bubbles with water, mess it around with a syringe, then pour the liquid into another medication bottle.

"There we go: the magical potion Jin Jin Cho is here!" I open the cap and offer the bottle to my father. "Daddy, do you have any pain in your body? Do you want some Jin Jin Cho?"

"No, thank you," replies my father as he rinses his hair. "I don't think I trust that medicine."

"Why not?"

"The name sounds strange and fishy!"

My father thinks Jin Jin Cho is inspired by my brother's heart medication, digoxin. But I swear, Jin Jin Cho is my original potion, a miracle that can cure any sickness in the world.

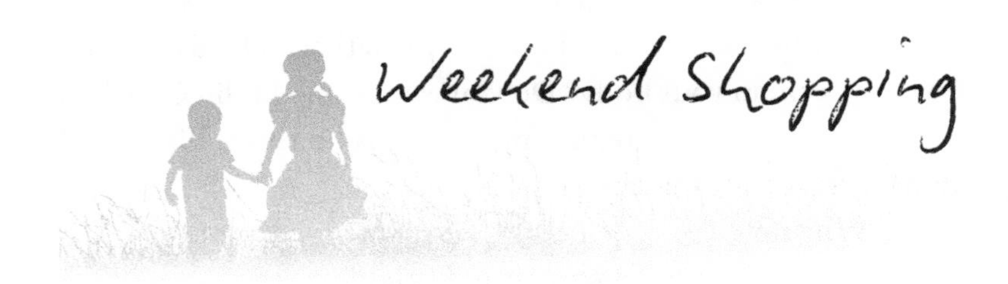

Weekend Shopping

A few weekends a month, my family drive to a large shopping mall in the suburb to buy things we cannot find in our neighbourhood shops. Once there, my mother handles the shopping with my brother in a shopping cart while my father takes me out for some fun activities.

My father and I always follow the same routine. First, we make a brief visit to the bookstore where my father buys a few books he's interested in. When he tells me I can also buy one, I pick a comic magazine for young girls – something my friends have, but my mother never buys for me.

We then go to the children's play section, Lan Lan Land, on the top floor where they have a merry-go-round, a small train ride, and other pieces of fun play equipment. We don't go inside, however. Instead, my father and I stop in front of the row of toy vending machine.

"Which one do you want to try?" my father asks.

I have two favourites. From one of them, I can get a big picture card of a scene from the anime series Sailor Moon. From the other one, I can get a super bouncing ball that comes in different colours and sizes. Once I decide which machine, I insert the coin my father gives me.

The fun part of this experience is that I don't get to choose which card or which ball, and I love the surprise that comes at the end. As the music plays from the machine, I wait in anticipation to see which picture card or which coloured ball will pop out of the dispenser.

Sometimes, I get the same one as I got before, and I'm a little disappointed. But sometimes, I'm rewarded with a particularly large bouncing ball or a picture card that I really like.

When this is all done, we move to our final destination, the burger shop Dom Dom, to enjoy the outcome of our treasure hunt over soft drinks.

My father and I sit at the first table by the window. He's gotten an oolong tea for himself and an orange juice for me. Once we're seated across from each other, my father takes out his new book from the paper bag, and I take the first sip of my orange juice.

The juice comes with a lot of ice cubes. As soon as the sweet liquid hits my tongue, I shiver at the sting of its coldness. While I'm immersed in the experience, I hear my father's laugh from the other side of the table.

"Your eyes!" He points at my eyes, chuckling. "They're closed!"

When I tell him I didn't close my eyes, my father asks me to take another sip. The moment I do, my eyes shut tight.

"There!" My father points at my eyes, laughing. "They're closed again!"

"I can't help it!"

"That's because the juice is cold."

My father seems to find my eye-closing reaction funny. And because he finds it funny, I also grin.

After some reading time over our drinks, we walk back to the car. My mother and brother aren't back yet, and we wait in the car, listening to the radio and reading our books some more. This is our weekend shopping routine.

America

One day, my mother tells me that Madoka and her family are moving to somewhere called America.

"America?" I repeat blankly.

I've heard of America in the kids' English program that I watch every day on TV. But it never occurred to me that it's a place we can actually visit.

"When will they come back?"

"Next year."

"Next year?"

Next year sounds like such a long time from now that I don't know what to think of it. *My friend is going to America and she'll come back next year.* I silently repeat that to myself as I wonder what it really means.

Before I know it, the day of their departure comes. All my friends and their parents stand near the community's entrance. An orange cab arrives, and my friend's family get inside. Madoka takes the furthest seat from us, so I cannot see her anymore.

As the cab starts, Madoka's mother and father wave at us from the open window. It feels like a scene from a storybook, all of us gathered to see my friend off like this.

The meaning of the grand farewell slowly becomes clear as the day goes by and we play without her. The next year is still far away, but I already miss her. And I keep wondering where on earth this place called America is.

These days, I'm interested in long hair. My hair isn't that long, barely reaching my shoulders, but I dream of having long hair like Sailor Moon.

In our tiny kitchen, there's a microwave sitting on a shelf. When I stand on a dining chair, my face comes right next to it, and there I see my reflection on the microwave door. In a home with no large mirror, any reflection of myself is a precious source of imagination.

One day, I stand on my chair and look in the microwave door as usual, checking my hair length. Then I dip my head slightly backward. To my delight, my hair now looks longer than it is. The girl in the reflection grins.

This becomes my secret ritual – to stand on my chair with a tilted head and measure my hair length in the microwave door.

One summer morning, I'm walking around our tiny apartment when I find my father still asleep in the back room. This room is where the four of us sleep at night and where my brother and I play during the day.

A pleasant wind comes in through the open window, creating waves in the worn-out curtains. My mother has already cleared away all the futons, and my father is sleeping on the floor with a thin blanket rolled around his stomach.

It's amazing how he's sprawled in the middle of the room, completely unaware of what's happening around him. I sit down and continue my observation when something unusual catches my attention. One of his arms sticks out behind his back at a strange angle. Moreover, his fingers are intersecting each other in a most complex way.

Curious, I try intersecting my own fingers like my father's. But no matter how hard I try, I cannot bring my fingers into the same position even though my fingers are much more flexible than his.

After several more attempts, I finally give up and go back to my morning exploration.

I love street-watching. Every day, I stand by the window of our back room and look out. Our apartment is on the second floor, and from this window, my familiar world looks different, more magical and exciting.

The view is always the same. The storage shack for the residents of my apartment block is right below my gaze, followed by a row of old cherry trees, then a street with local shopfronts. After that, there are rows and rows of roofs, and far down, I can see one tower sticking out from the sea of roofs.

As my gaze reaches the tower, my thought drifts off to my friend who's now in America. My mother told me America is somewhere very, very far.

I stretch up and focus on the tower sticking out from the roofs. And I wonder if America is even farther away than where that tower stands.

Another thing I love observing from the window is the sign boards of different shopfronts on the street. Right in front of our window is a small tofu shop run by an old lady, and when I stand by the window, its signboard comes at my eye level.

"University Potatoes" reads the sign. I know what a university is. There's one right behind our community and both my parents work there. But I have no idea what a university potato is. A few years later I finally learn that university potatoes is the name of a dish – deep-fried sweet potatoes coated with sweet sauce. Right now, I imagine a university potato to be a particular kind of potato that people eat at university.

After going through this chain of thought, I turn my attention to the entrance of the tofu shop. There I find the shopkeeper lady sitting by the entrance, smiling and waving at me.

"Why is she waving at me?" I feel offended, as if somebody had uncovered me during my secret world-watching project. So, instead of waving back at her, I hide behind the wall, out of her sight.

After some time, I poke out my head to check the situation. As soon as I'm back at the window, however, the shopkeeper lady waves at me again, smiling as broadly as ever. Apparently, she hasn't taken her eyes off my window.

The hiding and waving between us continues until somebody comes to the shop and the lady goes inside to serve the customer.

Yamaha Music School

Every week, my two best friends and I attend a group lesson at the Yamaha music school in the city centre. My mother and Sakura's mother take turns driving us all to the class. "All" consists of my two friends and me, our three little siblings, and three mothers. Nine of us cram into a five-seater and travel to our group lesson together.

The music school is housed on the top floor of the Yamaha music shop inside a shopping arcade. After about ten minutes, we arrive, and one by one, eight of us crawl out of the car before my mother drives it into the machine-operated parking tower.

There are two elderly men looking after the parking. Their jaws drop to the ground upon seeing us emerge from the tiny five-seater.

"Goodness!" They exclaim as we each land on our feet. "There are *more* coming out?!"

One day, my mother is driving us to the music school when a police car stops us. A kind-looking policeman approaches and peeks into the car – to see if my mother is wearing a seatbelt – as part of the routine checkup. She is. But that becomes his least concern as his gaze is met by nine eager pairs of eyes, then lands on what rests on my mother's back.

"Madam, you cannot drive with a baby on your back!" His kind voice hardens. "Yes, this car is overcrowded. But driving with a baby on your back? Absolutely not! You're risking your child's life!"

Because my mother is wearing a seatbelt, no fine is charged. After the remark, the policeman lets us go.

The next week, we're back to driving with nine people in the five-seater as if nothing has happened. But my mother no longer carries my brother on her back. Karen's mother holds him in her lap.

At music school, while we attend the group class, our mothers and little siblings sit on the floor along the wall and watch us. During the hour-long lesson, the little ones are given abundant snacks and told to stay quiet. But how can you expect them to stay still for so long?

Karen's sister and my brother share snacks and play together while Sakura's baby brother stays in his mother's lap. He doesn't yet walk or talk. But whenever he drops something, my brother comes along and picks it up for him.

One day, we're given a short melody and asked to expand it, adding harmony and making it into a full piece. I forget about my homework the moment I leave the classroom, my mind already busy with what fun things my friends and I will do after getting back home.

Every evening, after dinner, my mother reminds me. "Sweetie, it's your practice time," she calls out as she washes the dishes in the sink. "Do it now before you play with your brother."

My music practice typically lasts for about ten minutes. I play all the pieces I've learned in class on my digital piano, and by the time my mother finishes cleaning up the kitchen, my practice is also over.

But this week, I'm supposed to compose my own music. How do I do such a thing? I have no idea. It's only on the night before the lesson that my mother realizes I haven't done my homework yet.

"The lesson is tomorrow!" My mother's voice is raised. "You must do it NOW!"

After cleaning up the kitchen, my mother joins me in front of the piano and asks me what melody I can come up with that might go well with the given prompt.

"I don't know."

"You must think and try." My mother plays something on the piano. She's no musician, but she manages to come up with what sounds like a melody. "How about this?"

"That's good. I like it."

"Now what?" asks my mother, not at all discouraged by my less-than-eager response. "This is *your* homework. You need to think! What melody can come next?"

My mother and I grind our musical creativity for over an hour, and finally, we manage to produce a somewhat complete music piece. It's a very short one, with a simple development and a rather unexpected ending with a mysterious harmony. Though not sure about the quality, I'm happy I have something to show to my teacher.

The next day, in the group class, our teacher asks everybody to play the piece they've composed. When my turn comes, I play the piece my mother and I made with much struggle the night before.

"Oh, I like that ending," says my teacher as I finish playing. "That's interesting and unexpected!"

Everybody claps their hands, and I'm relieved my turn is over.

Most of my classmates' pieces are also short and simple except one. Karen, who loves piano, has composed a most intricate piece. After the prompt, her music turns into a lively waltz, reminding me of a picnic in a beautiful spring garden.

When the long and highly creative piece comes to an end, the whole room falls silent. Then I hear my mother whisper to Karen's mother. "Did she make this herself?"

"Yes," her mother replies, laughing. "Yes, she was so into it."

No further words come out of my mother's mouth. She's totally impressed. So am I. I'm amazed that someone can come up with such a gorgeous piece while my mother and I had to squeeze our musical talent to make a simple one.

Sailor Moon Dress

One day, Sakura shows up in a dress that looks like Sailor Moon's costume. "Mommy made this," she tells us when we ask her about it.

I cannot take my eyes off her. She looks like the *real* Sailor Moon. I want the dress, too, so that I can also become the real Sailor Moon!

As soon as I get back home, I tell my mother about Sakura's Sailor Moon dress. I explain to her how the dress looks like the one the real Sailor Moon wears. I hint that I also want one. But my mother brushes off my request.

"You already have the Sailor Moon wand and other toys," she points out. "That should be enough. You don't need a costume to be Sailor Moon!"

But I *want* the Sailor Moon dress even if I don't need one.

One day, my grandmother learns about my wish and sends me a brand-new Sailor Moon dress. My mother isn't impressed by it, but I'm over the moon with joy. I jump and dance around the house in ecstasy. Once I try it on, I declare I'm going to wear it every day.

"Of course not," says my mother without missing a beat. "This is a special dress, so you're only going to wear it on special occasions!"

To my heartbreak, the Sailor Moon dress is stored in the section of the wardrobe I cannot reach. Every day, I beg my mother to let me wear my Sailor Moon dress, but the request is rarely heard.

My friend wears her Sailor Moon dress all the time. Why can't I wear mine more often? It's so unfair, but I can't persuade my mother. I patiently wait for the occasions when I'm allowed to wear the dress.

One day, my mother gives me a permission to wear my Sailor Moon dress to my weekly music lesson. Nobody knows what it means for me to be able to put on this dress, to become the real Sailor Moon! I can hardly concentrate on anything during class. All I'm thinking about is my blue and white sailor dress.

An hour later, after we return home and it's time for me to play with my friends, I'm not yet ready to part with my dress. When my mother tells me to change into regular clothes, I refuse.

"No!" I shout. "I'm going to play in this dress!"

It's only been a few hours since I put on the dress, and if I give it up now, I don't know when I'll be able to wear it again.

"You must change," insists my mother. "Otherwise, your dress will get dirty."

"I won't get it dirty."

"But you will."

"No, I won't!"

Finally, my mother gives up. She allows me to play in the dress on the condition that I'll keep it clean.

"If you get it dirty" – her voice hardens, which should warn me of the risk I'm taking – "I won't let you in the house."

"I won't, I won't!"

I jump with excitement, my mother's warning already a distant noise. My mind is full of all the fun things I'll be doing with my friends while looking like the real Sailor Moon.

Sakura, Karen and I meet in the square playground and decide to play our favourite "Help Me!" game on the slide. Due to the rain earlier today, the ground is wet. The sandbox at the bottom of the slide is all muddy. For a second, my mother's warning rings in my mind.

"Let's go!" my friends call as they run up the slide, dragging me out of my stupor. "Help Me! starts now!"

I follow them up to the top, and with that, all my concern disappears. Now is not a moment to think about the mud. Now is all about having fun with my friends. And let me not forget, I'm Sailor Moon, strong and invincible!

Today, our "Help Me!" game escalates to a record level. It's more thrilling than usual because of the wet dirt. As we walk up and down on the slide barefoot, our feet catch the mud on the ground and soon the entire slide is covered with dirt.

At first, I try to stay away from the mud. But how is that possible when the whole slide is covered with it and our play is getting more and more exciting?

Once, as I slide down backwards screaming "Help!" I slip and land on my bottom. I vaguely become aware of the stain on my blue skirt. As I climb up the muddy slide, I realize that even my white shirt has gotten dirty.

If you get it dirty, my mother's voice echoes in my ears, *I won't let you in the house.*

Such a threat normally scares me, but not when I'm having a blast with my best friends. Now that my dress is stained, I'm less worried about making it dirtier.

A few hours later, when we finish our play, my dress is soaked in mud. There's not a spot that's not stained. My heart is still pumping from the excitement of the fun time, but as I walk up the staircase to my apartment alone, my head lowers and my steps become heavier. By the time I arrive at the door and ring the bell, my head is bowed like a criminal's in remorse.

"I TOLD YOU!" my mother snaps the moment she sees my muddy dress. "You're NOT allowed in the house! Stay right here and think about what you've done wrong!"

The door shuts in my face, leaving me alone in the hallway. I bang on the door, apologizing and pleading in vain. After a while, I sit down on the stair in front of the door, wondering why on earth I went out in my Sailor Moon dress and why on earth I wasn't more careful to keep it clean.

The sun has already set, and it's getting dark. The smell of supper fills the air. I sit there, all by myself, trying to distract my mind by paying attention to how cool the concrete step feels against my thighs. As time passes, I wonder what to do if my mother decides never to open the door. I could go to my friend's house and join their supper, maybe.

Suddenly, the door flings open, and my mother lets me inside. While my brother toddles around the living room like any other day, I'm escorted to the bathroom. My mother's still fuming, and I must explain to her exactly what I've done wrong. In my mind, I don't believe I've done anything wrong. My Sailor Moon dress is meant to be worn, and it's normal to get dirty sometimes. But I say none of this. Instead, I tell my mother how sorry I am to have gotten my dress dirty and that I won't do it again.

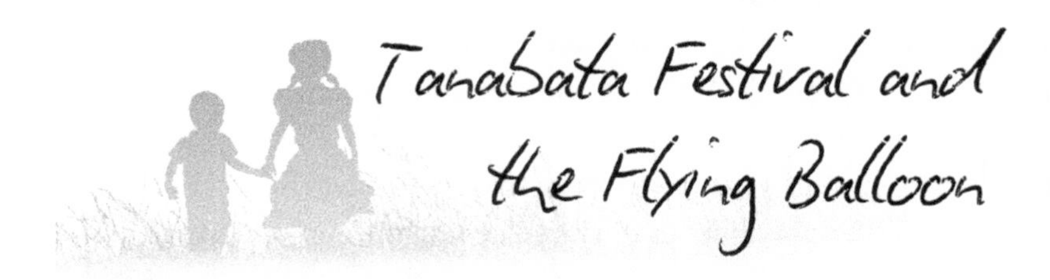

Tanabata Festival and the Flying Balloon

In early August, my maternal grandmother comes to stay with us for the *Sendai Tanabata* festival, our town's major summer attraction. From sixth to eighth August, all the stores inside the shopping arcades in the city centre hang traditional bamboo decorations from the outside ceiling, so visitors can walk through the dense forest of beautiful decorations while shopping.

This is the first time my one-year-old brother experiences this festival. Last August, he was still staying at hospital, thin and fragile. But now? He's a plump little boy, baby-talking and baby-walking.

My grandmother, mother, brother and I walk down the crowded passage of the familiar shopping arcade. The bamboo decorations are everywhere, their long paper tails caressing our faces as we make our way through them.

On the way, I find a vendor selling flying balloons. One of them has Sailor Moon on it.

"I want that balloon." The words fall from my lips, though I don't expect my wish to come true. It's not my birthday nor Christmas.

But today, something unexpected happens. As soon as I express my wish for the balloon, my grandmother speaks to the vendor and buys one for me. Within seconds, the very balloon I wanted lands in my hand.

"Hold on tight," she tells me. "So that it won't fly away!"

I'm so happy that for the rest of our walk, my Sailor Moon balloon is the only thing I think about. I watch the round, shiny pink balloon dance over my head as I walk and run through the curtains of bamboo decorations.

Once we're back home, I go to the back room and release the balloon from my hand. It shoots up to the ceiling, leaving its long thread dangling in the air. The balloon stays there the next day, and the day after, each day deflating a little, until one day, the air inside the balloon finally leaks out and both the balloon and the thread fall silently to the floor.

Midnight Ice Candy

Every night, before I sleep, my mother makes sure I go to the washroom. Despite that, I sometimes wet my bed. In my dream, just when I feel the need to pee, a toilet appears in a convenient location. The moment I sit on it and let go of my tension, however, a strangely warm sensation spreads under my back, waking me up to the reality that the toilet I sat on was a fantasy and that now my back is soaked with pee.

One summer night, I wake up from yet another toilet dream to a warm, wet mattress.

"Mommy!" I shake my mother sleeping next to me. "I've wet the bed!"

My mother gets up and brings me a set of fresh pajamas from the closet, and while I change, she places a thick layer of towels on the mattress to cover the wet spot. My mother, who scolds me for many things, never gets angry over a wet futon.

"When I was small, my mother would also help me whenever I wet the bed," my mother explains as she finishes placing the towels on the mattress and joins me in the living room, where I now stand in dry pajamas. "Without any complaints, she'd rearrange the futon so that I could sleep again."

I'm about to go back to sleep when my mother calls from the kitchen. "Do you want to eat a Popsicle?"

It takes a moment for my brain to understand what I've just heard. It's past midnight. My usually strict mother is offering me a Popsicle at this late hour when I've just wet the bed?

Without waiting for my reply, my mother takes out two Popsicles from the freezer. They're her favourite red bean flavour. "Want one?"

We sit together at the kitchen table and eat the Popsicles. My father and brother are fast asleep. The house is quiet. Since we haven't turned on the light, the kitchen is only dimly lit by the street lights from outside. The whole setting feels like a dream.

"This feels special," I say to my mother.

"It does, doesn't it?" she grins.

As we eat, my mother tells me more about the memory from her childhood when she wet the bed. How a toilet would appear in her dream just before waking up and how her mother was gentle with her when that happened. I listen intently.

When we finish eating, my mother tells me to go back to sleep. As I slip back under the warm blanket, I think about the secret Popsicle party I've just had with my mother, committing to my memory the excitement of this rare midnight snack.

Away from Home Again

In early October, my brother goes through another major heart surgery. I hear it's a follow-up to the big one he had after his birth, and that this time, things won't be as serious. But because my parents will both be busy looking after my brother, I'm once again sent to stay with my grandmother for three weeks.

My father and I travel to my grandmother's house together. As we get off the bullet train and change to a local train, my father buys me a package of candy at the station kiosk. While my mother strictly controls my snack intake, my father never cares about such matters. To my delight, he hands me the whole package.

At my grandmother's house, everybody eagerly waits for my arrival. Even my aunt who lives in a nearby city has come over to see me. When we arrive, my father joins everybody else at the table for tea and snacks, and they all spend some time chatting about my brother's condition, about me, and other things.

I'm too young to sit still, so I decide to explore my grandmother's big house with the candy in my hand. I've eaten a few on the trip, but now I eat one more. It's such a good feeling to hold the entire package of candies in my hand and be able to eat one whenever I want.

After a while, I come back to the dining room where adults are still talking. I come in through one door, pick a snack from the table, then exit from the other door. But before I exit, my aunt catches me.

"Hey, sweetie, why do I smell of something sweet from you?"

Of course, it's the candy in my mouth. But I won't say anything about it because this is *my* candy package, and I don't want anybody to take it away from me.

"Nothing, nothing!" I reply as I run toward the door. "You don't smell anything!"

Just as I exit, however, my father explains to my aunt. "She has a secret package of candies today."

I'm furious that my father has revealed my secret so easily, but I don't get to resent him for too long. Soon, I'm called as everyone gathers in the hallway to see my father off.

"Sweetie, be a good girl," my father reminds me. "Don't cause them trouble."

"Why would she?" others respond immediately. "She's such a wonderful girl. Aren't you, sweetie?"

I don't reply. I'm not interested in such pleasantry. All I think about is the fun adventure I'll have with my grandmother and how odd it feels that my father is going back home alone.

One day, my grandmother tells me she's going out to purchase a new one-wheel garden cart and asks me if I want to come with her. I have no idea what a one-wheel garden cart is, but knowing how exciting it always is to accompany her to a new place, I agree.

We walk to the nearest DIY store across the river. Today, a one-wheel cart is the only item on my grandmother's shopping list. She picks a green one, and we immediately head over to the checkout.

While waiting in line, my gaze roams the shelf in front of me and stops at the sight of a pink heart-shaped toy. My favourite anime character is beaming at me from the toy package. "Sailor Moon!" Before I know it, my hand reaches over to check what it is. It looks like a compact.

My grandmother is quick to notice my interest. "You want it?" Without waiting for my reply, she picks up the toy from the shelf and hands it to the cashier. "This as well, please."

Once we finish paying, we walk back home, pushing the brand-new cart in front of us. When we reach the bridge, however, my grandmother stops the cart and turns to me.

"Do you want to ride in the cart?"

"Ride in the cart?" My eyes widen with a mixture of disbelief and delight. Back home, my parents would never let me do such a fun thing! I eagerly climb into the shiny green cart.

We go back home like that, with my grandmother pushing the cart while I enjoy the ride. The scenery from the moving cart is fantastic. It feels like such a privilege to be moving without walking. As I'm carried on the cart, I open the toy my grandmother bought me. It's a heart-shaped compact that plays a tune whenever opened. I explain every detail of the toy to my grandmother as we travel.

This whole experience is so luxurious that as I watch the passing scenery around me, I'm convinced this is what it would feel like to be a princess.

My grandmother takes part in the community's senior folksong club. The group meets for regular practice at a nearby meeting house, and one evening, my grandmother takes me there with her.

As we leave home after dinner, it's already dark outside. My grandmother takes me through many narrow passages I never knew existed. We even walk past a bush behind somebody's house like ninjas. How amazing is it that my grandmother knows all these secret passages! Just when I'm absorbed in the ninja experience, we arrive at our destination.

The meeting house is clean and bright, with many kind faces welcoming us. They all seem to be near my grandmother's age. They sit in a circle with small tables in front of them to keep their songbooks.

We're the last members to arrive. My grandmother introduces me to everybody in the room. She explains to them that I'm staying with her for a few weeks while my parents are busy attending my little brother at hospital. I meet everybody's intent gaze and big smile.

As I sit next to my grandmother, she gives me a bag of candies. They're her favourite brand, Golden candy, and she carries them with her wherever she goes. Since I'll be spending the next couple of hours on my own, my grandmother gives me the entire bag.

As the song practice starts, I carefully observe all the people in the room, the way they sing and the way they chat with each other. It's interesting to see my grandmother interact with her peers. She looks different from when she is with her family members at home – fresh, lively, and somewhat free.

I also observe every detail of my grandmother's Golden candy. Amber coloured, the candy has the shape of a six-sided prism. I put it in front of my eyes to see if I can see through it.

While I play with the candies, other club members hand me theirs. Some of them also have the Golden candy, but unlike mine, which is plain, theirs have a tea flavour. Its colour is red. I play with both, noticing the difference and comparing their tastes.

The time passes very quickly. When the practice is over, we all pack our belongings and leave the meeting house.

As I follow my grandmother back home, through the narrow passages and past the bush behind somebody's house, I think to myself what an amazing evening we've had. In my hands are two bags of Golden candy, a precious souvenir from the night's adventure with my grandmother.

Every evening, when I brush my teeth next to my grandmother in the kitchen, she takes something out of her mouth and washes it under the running water in the sink.

"Grandma, what is it?" I ask her eagerly, trying to have a better look at the thing she's washing. "What are you washing there?"

"It's my false teeth," she replies, smiling at me.

"False teeth?" I repeat blankly. I've never heard of such a thing before. "What are they? Can I see them?"

"Well, sure." My grandmother sounds a little hesitant. "But I don't think you'll like them!"

When she shows me her false teeth, they look like real teeth. I'm impressed.

The next moment, something even more impressive happens. She puts the false teeth back into her mouth. My eyes widen in awe. My grandmother can take off and put on her teeth just like that!

The following day, I stand in front of a mirror examining my own teeth. I want to mimic what my grandmother did with her teeth last night, but unfortunately, I cannot take mine out of my mouth. As I search for something that can play the role of false teeth, I find a Hello Kitty toothbrush case. When I open it, its inside has a lot of indentations and reminds me of my grandmother's false teeth.

I run the water in the sink and wash the toothbrush case with my own toothbrush, all the while recalling the sense of wonder I felt as I watched my grandmother wash her false teeth under the running water.

One of my favourite spots to explore in my grandmother's house is the washroom. It's not a big space, but there's an interesting cabinet I love to observe in detail. Attached to the wall right next to the toilet, it comes at my eye level whenever I sit down for business.

The wooden cabinet door has a pattern resembling a staircase. When I open the door, toilet rolls and cleaning items come into my sight. Among them is a bottle of cleaning liquid, whose shape is narrow near the top and wide at the bottom. As I gaze at the bottle, an elegant princess slowly appears in front of me – the red round cap is her face and the bottle's blue body her dress, spreading gorgeously like a flower. The cabinet is her palace. It has many stories and rooms, and some of them are occupied by her attendants and servants.

"Where is the *prince*?"

As I wonder, somebody calls the princess from outside. It's the prince! The princess hurries down the staircase to meet the prince...

I bounce the bottle of cleaning liquid down the pattern on the cabinet door. The story always ends there. Sometimes, she goes out with the prince, and other times, she invites him inside the palace. But I never get to know what they do after that since that's when I stand up and leave the washroom.

There's an old shack in my grandmother's front garden where she stores her farming tools. Somebody told me that long ago the family lived there briefly while their house was being built. The shack is equipped with dish shelves, tables and a small fridge, all covered in dust.

On one of those tables, my grandmother often keeps onions, potatoes, and other hard vegetables taken from her vegetable garden. It's a fascinating view to find my grandmother's fresh vegetables among old, forgotten artifacts.

One day, when I go into the shack, a bunch of pumpkins welcome me on the table. They remind me of the Halloween pumpkins I've seen on the kids' English program on TV. I grab one and hurry back inside the house.

"Grandma, I want to make a Halloween pumpkin!" I exclaim as soon as I find my grandmother in the kitchen.

"A Halloween pumpkin?" She repeats blankly.

My grandmother has never heard of Halloween before. She doesn't watch the kids' English program. So, I explain to her that a Halloween pumpkin is a pumpkin with a face, and we can light a candle inside it.

"So, then we have to carve the pumpkin," says my grandmother, getting to her feet. "We'll need something sharp to take out the seeds and flesh."

The two of us sit at the kitchen table with the pumpkin to carve out the flesh with a knife. My grandmother tells me to watch while she does the hardest bit with the knife. I want to do it myself, but understanding the risk, I hold back, eagerly watching her work magic on the pumpkin. To my surprise, a lot of seeds come out of it. What a difference from the picture I've had in my mind – a candle inside a pumpkin!

Once all the seeds are gone, my grandmother lets me carve the face of the pumpkin. I make the eyes, the nose and the mouth, just like the pumpkin I saw on TV.

I want to pierce completely through the pumpkin so that the eyes, nose, and mouth are connected to the inside, but the skin is too thick for me to do that. So, when I finish, even though it looks like a Halloween pumpkin, a candle cannot be lit inside. I'm a little sad about it, but my grandmother, who doesn't know how a real Halloween pumpkin looks, is happy with the outcome.

"There we go, your Halloween pumpkin!"

My smiley Halloween pumpkin sits in the shack with other pumpkins until the end of my stay.

Wedding

Shortly after the successful completion of my brother's heart operation when I'm back home with my family, I hear that one of my older cousins is getting married and that I'll be going to his wedding with my father. The whole family have been invited, but since my brother needs to rest at home after his surgery, my mother stays behind with him.

I've only read about weddings in my storybooks. I don't know what to think of it except that I'm excited about the travelling part. Since the wedding takes place near my grandmother's house, we take the bullet train. My mother has dressed me in a midnight blue velvet dress. Wearing it makes me feel like a princess.

The wedding ceremony is followed by a reception. There's a short waiting period between them, and while my father and I stand in the lobby, somebody takes a picture of us. Instead of smiling like I normally do, I pose like a princess from my storybook, with tightly pressed lips and my hands crossed in the back.

At the reception, I'm seated between my father and my aunt at one of the round tables. My gaze is glued to the bride and her beautiful dress. I wonder why the groom – my cousin – doesn't wear something as gorgeous. The bride first appears in a white dress, then later changes into a bright red dress, both so dreamy and breathtaking.

Toward the end of the party, a staff member calls me and a young boy of my age. "Okay, little ones," she tells us with a beaming smile. "The bride and the groom have special gifts for you. Upon my signal, you'll walk up to them and hand them these flowers, okay?"

The boy looks as puzzled as I am, but I bet he likes the idea of a gift as much as I do. When the staff member gives us a nod, we eagerly walk up to the front stage. The boy goes to the bride and I go to my cousin. With a big smile, my cousin hands me two boxes.

"One for you, one for your little brother."

That little comment not only feels natural, but makes me proud. A reminder that I'm now a big sister even though my brother isn't with me today.

When I open one box, a big red toy car with Mickey Mouse on the driver's seat comes out. The content of the other box is exactly the same. I've never been a car person, but I love *this* one. I like its round shape and the fact that it's a gift.

Back home, my brother is excited to have his toy car. He follows me around holding his red car while I carry mine. We run around the living room with our first matching toys in our hands until our father tells us to calm down.

Later that evening, I pick up a black marker and write my name on one car and my brother's name on the other – the first of many more name-writings to come.

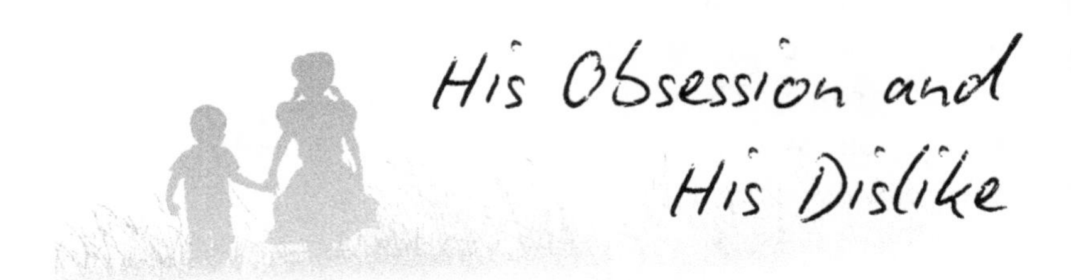

His Obsession and His Dislike

Ever since my one-year-old brother started to walk, he's developed a particular obsession: buses. Whenever a bus passes by, his whole body turns in its direction while his wide-eyed gaze is fixed on the large vehicle. "Bus! Bus!" My brother repeats it enthusiastically until the bus is out of sight.

Our town has two kinds of bus services. One is operated by the city, and the other by the prefecture. The city buses are green with blue stripes while the prefecture buses are white with red stripes. Whenever he sees a bus, my brother carefully checks which kind of bus it is and never forgets to mention it to everyone around him.

When my brother stayed at the large hospital, my mother and father each bought him a few metal toy buses modelled after the city and prefecture buses. Now, they're becoming my brother's most treasured toys, accompanying him wherever he goes.

One weekend evening, we're at a family diner to grab a quick dinner. I ask for my favourite drink – a glass of melon soda, the green sparkling liquid topped with vanilla ice cream. As soon as

I take a sip from the straw, its tingly sensation fills my mouth and I close my eyes with a smile.

On the other side of the table, my brother sits in a highchair, waiting for his food. He watches me closely, then makes a noise, stretching his hand toward my melon soda.

"Sweetie, are you sure you want it?" my mother asks him in surprise. "It's not the kind of juice you normally have. It's bubbly."

My brother doesn't budge. So, the glass of melon soda is passed to the other side of the table where my brother eagerly takes a sip from the straw.

The moment the drink enters his mouth, however, he frowns. He then quickly sticks out his tongue and brushes it with his hand many times, as if to remove the tingly sensation from his tongue. My brother continues his funny brushing movement, and we all burst into laughter.

"He doesn't like sparkling juice!" my father chuckles, sliding the glass back to my side of the table.

Now it's my turn to watch my brother curiously. *How come he doesn't like bubbly drinks? They're the best thing in the world!*

This is the first time I discover my brother's dislikes that are different from mine.

Monday and Thursday mornings are when my mother goes out for work, and my father, brother and I stay at home together. Having finished breakfast before our mother left home, my brother and I spend some time watching TV while my father gets up and eats breakfast over the newspaper. Once he's ready, the three of us go to the back room.

"What do we do today?" asks my father, and I bring out a box of wooden blocks.

"I'm going to make a castle," I say, spreading the blocks on the floor. "A gorgeous castle like you've never seen!"

With that, I dive into my castle-building. I have so many wonderful designs in my mind, inspired by all the picture books I've been reading.

As I build my castle using different shapes – cylinders for the pillars, rectangles and squares for the walls, triangles and semicircles for the roof – my little bother works on his project next to me. He's making a bus, his current obsession. He picks up two circles, then places a rectangle on top of them.

"Bus!" My brother beams with a smile as he points to his creation. "Bus!"

Next to my three-dimensional castle stands my brother's two-dimensional bus. My brother has used only two shapes. He's not interested in using other shapes at all?

My father suggests that he make something else, but my brother is so content with his two-dimensional bus that he doesn't bother.

Magical Nights

One day, I hear about a Sailor Moon movie coming to the theatres in my town. I have little idea what a movie is, but I want to go because it's about my favourite anime character. I cannot miss it.

My father agrees to take me to the movie. After an early dinner, the two of us leave my mother and brother at home and catch a bus to the city centre. We walk through the shopping arcade for some time before stopping in front of an elevator.

"Are we there yet?" I ask impatiently.

"Almost," my father replies. "It's upstairs."

When the elevator carries us somewhere high up and the door opens, my heart skips a beat. Who could have imagined that it leads to a gorgeous room with red carpets and yellow sparkly lights?

I follow my father onto the thick red carpet. The attendant at the ticket counter tells us the movie has just started. My father and I run into the theatre and sit on the nearest seating we find, right in front of the screen.

For a second, my mind is blown by the huge screen that stretches across the whole front wall. But then what's happening on the screen becomes more important. The story quickly absorbs me. Unlike the usual weekly episodes, in this movie, the enemy is stronger, and Sailor Moon and her team struggle to locate the evil force while many children are abducted from their town, including Sailor Moon's little sister.

Tightly holding the edge of my seat, I follow the story with a pounding heart. It's so thrilling that I can hardly breathe.

Eventually, however, Sailor Moon and her team beat the enemy and the story comes to a happy ending. Lights come back to the theatre, announcing the intermission before the next story begins.

My father and I stroll out to the lobby, my head still throbbing from the thrill of the adventure I've just watched. I sit on one of the red cushioned armchairs along the wall while my father leaves for the washroom.

I'm recalling each scene in detail as my pulse finally slows down when my father calls my name.

"Sweetie!" I look up to find him shuffling my way with a beaming smile. He's carrying something. "Let's have popcorn!"

Never in my life have I seen such a huge cup of popcorn, or of any snack, if it comes to that. I cannot imagine my mother buying it for me.

"Do you think Mommy will like the popcorn?" I say my concern out loud, thinking that we might be scolded later when she finds out. But my father isn't worried.

"Mommy isn't here," he grins. "She wouldn't understand the fun of popcorn! We'll eat this, and she won't know about it!"

I grin back, and we spend the rest of the intermission and the next part of the show munching popcorn from the huge paper cup. I cannot tell which I enjoy more – the movie or the huge cup of secret popcorn.

One winter evening, I come home after playing with my friends outside. While I wait for supper, I sit on the floor of our tiny living room next to the couch and play with my dolls.

The usual kids' program is blasting from the TV, and my little brother is playing behind me. My mother is cooking in the kitchen. I ignore all the noises, trying to concentrate on the story in my head. But today, my eyes are heavy. Before long, I drift off to sleep, with my head propped against the couch.

When my eyes open again, the house is very quiet, and I don't know how long I've slept like that. The TV is off, and I don't hear my little brother's voice anymore. *Where is supper?* I sit up, wondering what's going on, when my mother comes in.

"Oh, are you awake?" She smiles at me, then goes back to the kitchen. There is a sound of her putting something in the microwave, followed by a beep.

"Where is supper?" I ask.

"We finished supper a long time ago," my mother replies. "You've been sleeping for quite a while." She says it's already past midnight.

My mother brings me a bowl of rice and a small plate with a few pieces of fried chicken flavoured with lemon and garnished with a single piece of lettuce.

"Your brother was calling your name," says my mother as she watches me eat the food. "But you didn't hear him, did you?"

"No, I didn't," I answer, picturing my brother sitting next to me and trying to catch my attention. Too bad I didn't get to respond to him. He must have wanted to play with me.

As I eat my late dinner, a sense of happiness fills my heart. There's nothing fancy about the food, but the way it was kept and microwaved for me at this late hour makes it feel like a special feast.

"This is *delicious,*" I tell my mother. "Really delicious."

"That's good," smiles my mother, sitting next to me and watching me eat.

My mother is unusually kind tonight. I wonder why she didn't wake me up for supper in the first place because that's what she'd normally do.

But I don't ask. I want the magic of the evening to last longer. I don't want to risk anything that might break it. I'm only happy that my mother has kept this special dinner for me after everybody else went to bed.

Skating

One winter day, during one of our regular visits to the mall, my father tells me that we are going to skate today.

"Skate?" I repeat blankly. "What's skating?"

"You'll see," says my father. "It's going to be fun. You'll love it!"

We enter the shopping mall as usual, but instead of taking the familiar way, my father leads me in a different direction. After walking through sections of the mall I've never seen before, we come to a deserted corridor. There's no more background music, no more shopping displays here, but just a plain corridor. We walk down a spiral staircase, into a narrow corridor with orange walls.

Suddenly, a reception desk appears in front of us. My father asks the receptionist something, and when he calls me to follow him again, he carries an armful of bulky items.

"These are our skates and protective gear," he explains as he hands me a bright pink pair of gloves. "And these are your gloves."

The sight of the skating rink is nothing like I've imagined: a spacious flat white surface glimmering under the bright white light. My father says it's all made of ice, but it looks nothing like the ice cubes I'm used to seeing at home.

My father helps me to change shoes in the seating area next to the rink. These ice skates… they're so hard to walk in! I try not to lose my balance as I wobble after my father toward the entrance to the rink.

Though not an expert, my father knows how to skate. He tells me to stay close to the railing since I'm not yet able to stand on the ice, then he teaches me the basics – how to stand on the ice without losing my balance, how to bend my knees, how to angle my feet, how to push against the ice to glide, and even how to fall properly.

After the lecture, my father skates around the rink by himself while I practice on my own.

I practice with total concentration. I want to be able to move on the ice like the others around me. First, I learn to stand on the ice without falling. I then travel around the rink following the railing. By the end of our time, I manage to walk around the whole rink with the help of the railing. That feels like a great accomplishment.

A few weekend sessions pass like that, and one day, my father and I are back on the rink. Though I'm now able to walk on the ice without support, I still don't dare to steer away from the railing. I keep circling the rink along the railing, enjoying the feeling it brings.

After some time, my father leaves the rink to sit and rest. He suggests I do the same, but too eager to practice, I decline the offer. Just as I move toward the railing to resume my practice, a voice calls out to me. When I turn, I come face to face with a girl who looks a few years older than me.

"Hey!" The girl, dressed in a white costume, smiles up at me. "Let's skate together!"

I've seen this girl skate. She's a skilled skater whose movements are smooth and graceful. I don't think I'll make good company for her.

"I can't," I mumble to her. "I can't skate well..."

"Don't worry," the girl smiles again, extending her arm. "Let's go!"

Before I can protest any further, she takes my hand, and off we go.

The moment we start, all my fear disappears. My body becomes light, and I feel as if we are flying in the sky. Together, we cross the rink from edge to edge, side to side. We make curves on the ice, and as we speed on, the cold wind caresses our faces. After making a full circle, we come back to the spot where we started.

"Great job!" the girl cheers me with a big smile before we part ways.

I'm still dazzled from the flight I've just taken as I leave the rink to join my father in the seating area. As soon as I sit down, he exclaims, "You're skating beautifully!"

I try to explain to him how magical the whole experience has been, but I realize no words can capture that sensation. Only I can remember the magic I've experienced with the girl.

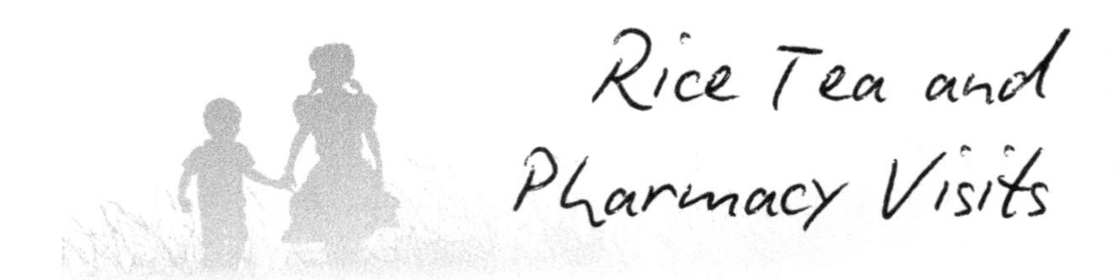

Rice Tea and Pharmacy Visits

Once a month, my brother goes to the large hospital for a regular checkup on his heart condition, and I often accompany him and our mother. In the early morning, we drive to the hospital, and once the checkup is done, we collect a few prescribed medications at a pharmacy across the street.

The pharmacy is on the ground floor of a brand-new building. The spacious waiting area is neatly lined with rows of comfortable benches. As soon as my mother settles on one of them, my brother and I venture out to explore the room.

It's very quiet here. There are no kids except us, and the only sound I can hear are people's distant chattering voices behind the counter and the low sound coming from the TV screen in front of the benches.

As we continue our exploration, we stumble upon a machine with a stack of tiny paper cups next to it. When I press one of the buttons, hot liquid comes out from the tap. I quickly place a cup underneath it and press the button again. The liquid is light brown.

"It's tea!"

I help my brother pour some tea in his cup, too. Together, we sit down on one of the benches and sip our tea. This tea has a roasted flavour, and I like it. It's so much more delicious than the usual green tea!

My brother and I make multiple trips to the tea dispenser, helping ourselves to the brown tea until our mother calls us to head back home.

Yamaha Music Showcase

March arrives, and the annual Yamaha music showcase takes place in a concert hall outside the city centre. It's been a year since our group class started. This is an occasion for us to perform in front of our family members and show them how much progress we've made.

We've prepared many music pieces for the concert. They're a combination of singing and Electone performances. While some of us play the Electones, others sing. Or sometimes, it's our teacher who plays an Electone, and we all sing in unison. All of this happens on stage.

I've dreamed of wearing a princess-like dress for this showcase, but when my mother brings me my stage costume, it's a rather plain checked jumper skirt to be worn with a white blouse. She puts a white bow on top of my regular half-up hair. Again, not so princess-like. But this will have to do.

At the venue, I'm joined by Sakura and Karen along with other classmates all dressed up. My eyes are immediately glued to Sakura's costume. Made of shiny red and gold material, the dress is shaped like a traditional Japanese kimono. She says her mother made the dress for this occasion, impressing everybody in the lobby.

Our stage time is short, but because it's our first big performance, we're all excited and nervous. We sing songs and play the Electones, trying our best to perform as nicely as when we practiced. The audience – our parents, grandparents and younger siblings – applauds each time we finish a piece.

When our performance is over, I play with Sakura and Karen in the lobby. My brother, Karen's little sister and Sakura's baby brother also follow us around. Our mothers take pictures of us. Then it's time for family photos. Mothers take turns capturing each family with a camera.

When my family's turn arrives, the four of us line up in front of the wall, my mother holding my brother in her arms and my father placing his hand on my shoulder.

None of us knows that this will forever be the only photograph that captures my complete family of four.

Part 3

Ordinary Days

(April 1995 – March 1996)

Castella Cake and a Hospital Visit

In early April, my little brother is diagnosed with pneumonia and admitted to the hospital. My mother accompanies him. This is not the large hospital he visits to have checkups on his heart condition, but the one where he was born and where we all go when we catch a cold. Staying at this hospital means that things are under control.

Nonetheless, my father and I go to visit them often. One morning, he puts me on the back of his bike, and together we head off to the city centre.

On the way, we make two stops. The first is at an outdoor rummage sale at the local YMCA, where my father buys a few books for himself and gets a red heart plush toy for me. The second is at a local sweet shop close to the hospital. My father buys one Castella cake – a yellow Japanese sponge cake – as a gift for my mother and brother.

My brother's staying in a small private room with my mother. Upon our arrival, he gets so excited that he jumps on his bed, and my mother has to remind him to stay still since he's hooked up to an IV.

As we settle down, my mother brews tea, and my father tells her about the rummage sale we've been to.

"Look what I've got!" I show my mother the new red heart plush. "It's so smooth and cute. I'm so lucky I found this because it's my favourite!"

After that, my father takes out the box of Castella cake, and my mother potters around looking for a knife and plates. I'm delighted that we'll soon be eating the treat together.

A moment passes, and I turn around to call my brother when I realize something has changed. The bedsheet, which I thought was white, is now drenched in red…

"Mommy! Daddy! Look!" I shriek. "The bed is red!"

Immediately, my mother presses the intercom on the wall, and in no time, a nurse appears at the door. She quickly readjusts the needle on my brother's hand and changes the bedsheets.

Once she's gone, I ask my parents what happened.

"The needle got removed from your brother because he moved around too much," they reply calmly as if nothing is out of order. "But it's all settled. Now, let's eat the cake!"

But my concern only grows bigger.

"So, that was *his* blood then?" I press. "The bed was all red. How much blood came out of him?"

My parents repeat that there's nothing to worry about and hand me my portion of the Castella cake. But sadly, my appetite is gone. All I can think of is that bright red bedsheet covered with my brother's blood. Even my new heart plush is now a reminder of that. Next to me, my brother helps himself to the cake as if nothing happened.

Sailor Moon

Sometime in the spring, a new Sailor Moon series comes out on TV. This time, the spotlight of the story is on Sailor Moon's little sister Chibi Moon. She comes in contact with a winged horse who is chased by the dark force. A magical object called the Stallion Rêve appears in Chibi Moon's attic room, and she uses it to talk with the winged horse.

Every Saturday at 7 pm, I sit in front of the TV to watch the new episode. I know all my girlfriends are also doing the same. What I watch today will become part of our play when we meet next time. Sailor Moon is our heroine. Our world revolves around Sailor Moon.

Kindergarten

In early April, I attend a welcome party at my kindergarten. It's a party organized for us new kindergarteners by our teachers, and it's separate from the official entrance ceremony. We children occupy the front rows of the small auditorium while the parents stay in the backseats. My mother isn't among them. She was here though, for the official ceremony. Today, she has something else to attend and couldn't come. She told me this one was going to be an informal party and I should be okay without her.

Not that I worry about it. I'm quite used to being on my own.

As soon as the party begins, I get busy following all the songs and games our teachers have prepared for us. Clapping my hands, laughing, singing, I'm having the best time with everybody else in the room.

After a round of fun, however, an announcement is made. All the new kids are invited to come on stage with their mother or father to play a game together. As everybody around me stands up and walks to the front with their parents, I suddenly feel anxious. I don't have my mother or father with me. Not sure what to do, I follow the crowd onto the stage alone.

We're told to stand face to face with our parent to play a hand game. I stand at the far end of the stage, staring at the empty space in front of me.

The music starts and I look around uncertainly.

Just when I decide to use my imagination and pretend somebody is standing in front of me, a young lady teacher comes running and kneels before me. With a big smile, she takes my hand and plays the game with me. Even though I feel anxious and don't smile at her, she keeps smiling and talking to me. When the music stops and the audience cheers, she gently brings me back to my seat.

Later, when I go back to my home class, I'm surprised to see her again. She'll be our homeroom teacher for the year, and that's when I learn her name: teacher Mina.

One late spring day, we get a pamphlet at kindergarten about a Sailor Moon exhibition happening in town. The exhibition quickly becomes the most exciting conversation topic among the girls. Every day, somebody shares the story of their visit to the exhibition. Apparently, different character mascots from the anime series are present at the event.

"Who did you meet there?" we eagerly ask whoever has visited the exhibition.

Someone has been lucky to meet Sailor Moon herself, and others have met Sailor Jupiter or Sailor Venus or other sailor warriors. These stories are so impressive that I cannot wait to go there myself.

A few weeks into the exhibition, I finally get permission. My father has agreed to take me there while my mother stays with my little brother.

The exhibition is on the edge of town, and my father and I take the subway. All along the way, I'm nervous that I won't get to meet Sailor Moon. "Do you think Sailor Moon will be there, Daddy?" I don't know how many times I ask him on the subway. "Oh, I really hope she's there today!"

"We'll see when we get there."

The exhibition is happening on the second floor of the building. As we get off the escalator, we're surrounded by walls of illustrations from the Sailor Moon anime series. They're nice, but not what I'm looking for.

"There she is, sweetie! Your Sailor Moon!"

I turn around upon hearing my father's cheerful voice, excitement bubbling in my heart. He's pointing to a large character standing at the far end of the hall. This character, however, has pink hair instead of yellow.

"Daddy, that's not Sailor Moon." My voice sinks in disappointment. "That's Chibi Moon!" Because my father isn't a follower of the Sailor Moon series, every character looks the same to him.

I look around to see if there are any other characters in the room. But she's the only one. I'm sad Sailor Moon isn't here today, though I'm happy to see Chibi Moon. She's also a popular one.

"Let's go closer." My father nudges me, and we walk toward the character.

This Chibi Moon is gigantic. She's taller than my father. Even though she acts friendly, her size scares me. I stop several feet away, my cautious gaze trained on her.

"Aren't you going to say hello to her?" my father asks me while other children come around and interact with Chibi Moon. I tell him I'm scared. "What? Scared?" He laughs. "What's there to be scared of?"

But no matter what he tells me, I remain unmovable. We stand there like that for a while. Then, my father surprises me by saying it's time for us to leave.

"Your mother and brother are waiting for us at home. We need to get going."

"Already?" I glance at Chibi Moon once again. Nobody is around her. She's watching me, waving as if to invite me closer.

"Are you sure you don't want to say hello to her?" my father asks me for one last time.

I'm still anxious, but it would be a shame not to greet her after coming all this way. So I muster up my courage and walk up to the character. Towering over me, she takes my hand in hers. Enormous, yet incredibly soft hands.

As we leave the hall and descend the escalator, I cannot hide my excitement.

"She wasn't scary," I repeat breathlessly. "She wasn't scary at all! Her hands were soft!"

My father laughs. "Of course not. What made you think she was scary in the first place?"

The next day, I proudly announce to my friends at kindergarten that I've met Chibi Moon at the exhibition and shaken hands with her. I also add how soft her hands were.

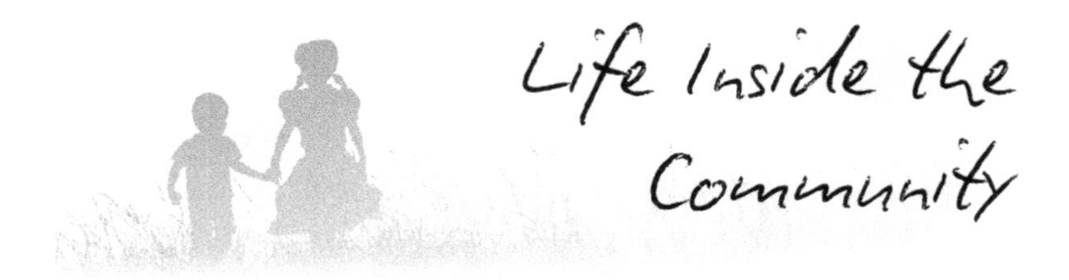

Life Inside the Community

April turns into May. As the pale pink cherry blossoms rain on the ground and the baby green leaves appear on the tree branches, a new excitement arrives in our community – the swallows.

Just outside of our community, among the neighbourhood shops, is a meat shop called Endo. One day, on our way back from kindergarten, somebody calls out. "Look, birds' nests!"

When I look up, there are a few places right under the roof of the Endo meat shop where round things are attached. I've never seen birds' nests before, only heard of them in my storybooks.

"What birds?" somebody asks.

"Those are swallows," one of the adults replies. "They're laying eggs inside the nests!"

A few birds fly back and go inside the round objects under the roof. I'm surprised to see the elegant way in which these black birds fly. What a difference from the crows! I'm also surprised that there's enough space inside for these birds, because the nests don't look large.

"Swallows?"

In Japanese, swallows are called *tsubame*. The word is a little hard to pronounce correctly. My little brother, whose eyes eagerly follow the birds, calls them *tsunabe*.

Everybody's gaze is now fixed on the birds flying in and out of the nests.

"They're parent birds," somebody explains. "They're protecting their eggs. Soon there will be baby birds!"

From that day on, watching the swallows under the roof of the Endo meat shop becomes our ritual. Over the next few weeks, we see one of the nests attacked and destroyed by crows. We then watch little heads of chicks peeking from the remaining nests, their mouths opening and closing eagerly for food. Quickly, the chicks grow into birds with black feathers and white tummies. They practice flying, and in no time, we find the nests empty.

"When will they come back?" somebody asks.

"We'll see them again next year," an adult's voice answers. "Let's hope they'll come back here!"

At home, my brother keeps talking about his *tsunabe*. He already looks forward to seeing them again next summer.

One evening, my parents mention to us a night festival taking place at our neighbourhood's Shinto shrine. As night falls, the sound of drums starts in the distance, enveloping us with a sense of excitement.

After dinner, the four of us walk to the festival. As we get closer, the sound becomes louder, and many red lanterns come into view. It seems we've arrived in the middle of the community's karaoke contest. Somebody is singing on the pop-up stage. This singer, whoever she is, is really good. Waving her hips, wagging her fingers at the audience with a big smile, this lady performs like someone on TV.

There are monitor screens on both sides of the stage showing the singer from close up. The moment I see her face, my heart skips a beat.

"Oh my!" Next to me, my mother also gasps in disbelief.

That's Sakura's mother on stage! Dressed in a sparkling show costume, moving and singing on the stage, she looks so different from the person I see every day. This lady is in the zone. She's the star of the night!

"Look at her!" my mother cheers at the stage. "Look at her! She's amazing!"

When the performance finally comes to an end, we all clap our hands hard in awe.

The next morning, my brother and I run about our tiny apartment restlessly. Today is the day of the *Mikoshi* festival. We'll be walking down the streets with other kids in the neighbourhood carrying a *mikoshi*, a wooden box believed to carry a god inside.

Last year, it was just me from my family, but this year, my little brother is also participating. He's turning two in June, now old enough to march along with the others. My mother helps us both put on the blue festival vests and put twisted towels on our heads. I march around the room checking my cool festival look.

My little brother is also excited, but for a different reason. He's happy because he feels like a big boy being able to participate in the festival with me and the other older kids.

Once ready, we go out to meet up with others from the neighbourhood. Parents stay on the side while all the children gather around the *mikoshi*. Following the instruction of the festival master, we carry it together.

"*Wasshoi! Wasshoi!*" we chant in a loud voice as we march down the street in a line. "*Wasshoi! Wasshoi!*" I walk with my two best friends while my brother follows in the back with other little kids. After some time, we come to the end of the street, steaming under the warm sun.

The festival master comes around and claps his hands, telling everyone how well we've done the walk. Now it's time for a treat. Adults walk between us, handing out cans of cold juice to our now impatient hands. As soon as I get mine, I open the can and take a sip. The touch of the cold drink on my tongue is so refreshing that I feel all the walk was worth it.

Later, back home, my brother and I are still intoxicated by the festival magic, talking endlessly about the day, refusing to remove our costumes. Finally, my mother tells us to wait for the next year. "It's done for today, sweeties. You'll do it again next year!"

I know she's just distracting us. But her words make my brother's smile bigger.

"We'll do it again next year!" he says again and again, showing everybody his festival costume until my mother finally grabs him and takes it off.

Right next to the entrance of my apartment building, there's an old empty oil drum sitting by the wall. Nobody knows why it's there, who placed it there or when. The metal drum is so rusty that it has turned reddish brown.

One day, I'm playing with Sakura and Karen in the back of my apartment block when, out of curiosity, I approach the forgotten oil drum to take a closer look. There's a round hole on top. I press my eye against it to have a peek.

Inside, the oil drum is completely dark, reminding me of the night sky. As I continue to watch, I see something sparkling at the bottom. "I can see stars!" I exclaim.

My two friends join me, and they confirm that they can also see the stars.

"This oil drum is a planetarium!" We dance around the rusty drum, celebrating our wonderful new discovery. "We have our own planetarium here!"

In the square playground in front of my apartment, there's a basket swing. It's a swing shaped like a basket where four people can sit. There was a time when we used to sit inside the basket and our parents gently pushed the swing for us.

But those sweet days are long gone. These days, my two best friends and I play aggressively on the swing. Two of us push the swing from both sides as fast as possible while the third person crouches inside the basket, trying to maintain her balance.

One sunny day, we're playing on the basket swing as usual. I'm one of the pushers, and each time the basket swings to my side, I tackle it with all my force. The basket starts to swing higher and faster, and I push it with even more force.

Suddenly, I hear a voice behind me. Some of the mothers are chatting nearby, and they've mentioned my name. For a split second, my focus is stolen by the conversation, and I forget about the swing altogether.

"Watch out!" Karen's voice grabs me out of my stupor. "It's coming!"

I turn around just when the heavy metal basket has swung in my direction at full speed.

Bang! The basket crashes into my face with such force that no thought comes to my mind. All I can feel is the sharp pain on my chin. When my brain registers that I've been hit by the swing, tears stream down my face.

Everybody rushes to me while I cry helplessly out of sheer shock. "You're bleeding." Karen's mother examines my injury. "We'll take you to your mother." Covering my chin with tissue, she and another mother escort me back to my home, which is just around the corner from the playground.

The next thing I know, my mother shoves me into the car, and we head off to visit the nearest clinic. As we pass the playground, I see my friends and their mothers standing at the entrance, their faces clouded with worry. I cannot help but wonder why such an accident had to happen. Just a moment ago, I was having a blast with my friends. Now I'm pulled away from all the fun, heading to see a doctor.

The clinic is an old house down the hill, not at all looking like a hospital. But the doctor gives me proper treatment, stitching up the wound. It turns out the injury was a minor one, but I'm warned that the scar might last for a lifetime.

Adventure of Two

I love playing with my dolls. It's my favourite solo activity in the world, and whenever I'm not playing with my friends, I'm found sitting with my dolls, engaged in a long, emotional drama with them. I always improvise the story, and as I act out each new storyline, I smile and cry with my characters.

My little brother, on the other hand, has little interest in dolls. Instead, he's a lover of buses and owns a large collection of toy buses. Whenever he's alone, he sits with his toy buses, carefully moving them around, mimicking the buses in the real world. What's most important to him is that his buses travel around the room with precision. It usually doesn't involve much story.

One morning, I'm playing with my dolls as usual in the back room of our tiny apartment. It's another emotional story, and after some time, I need to take a break to reflect on what's happened so far.

As I put down my dolls and become silent, I hear somebody else's voice nearby. It's my brother. He's sitting across from me with his toy buses. But today, something is different. His toy buses are talking, playing out a drama.

A few buses are stationed on top of a large yellow tin box. They seem to be on an adventure together when suddenly, one of them falls off the edge. I quickly turn to the other buses, expecting them to say something to the poor one who's just fallen off the cliff.

"Ooh!" My brother moves one of the buses on the clifftop. "Are you okay?"

No, of course not. It was a big fall. He or she must be injured.

"Yes, I'm all right," a calm reply echoes from the bottom of the cliff.

"You should come back!" the bus on the clifftop says, no sense of urgency in his voice. "Do you need help?"

Yes, of course! Please help them! I eagerly wait for the next line but my brother looks up, noticing my gaze. With a sheepish smile on his face, he stops talking and remains quiet.

So I return to my dolls to resume their emotional drama. My brother's buses also resume their conversation. Soon, however, I become so absorbed in my own story that I don't hear anything else in the room anymore.

It's another ordinary morning in our apartment. Invited by the sunny weather outside, my brother and I go out on a morning exploration by ourselves.

We walk down the staircase and step outside of our building. I take my brother to my planetarium, the large, empty rusted oil drum right next to the entrance. I want to show him how the shiny spots inside look like stars in the night sky.

When I reach the oil drum, however, I see something big and hairy dangling in the air between the oil drum and the wall.

"Yikes! A spider!" I scream and jump behind my toddler brother. He stands tall in front of me, without the slightest hint of fear on his face. He picks up a stick from the ground and swings it at the cobweb like a sword.

"Ei! Ei!" he shouts like a brave warrior as he continues to swing the stick between the oil drum and the wall. The poor spider drops to the ground and disappears from our sight.

Our morning exploration is over. We run up the stairs and go back inside, excited to tell all the details of our brief adventure to our mother.

These days, I'm really into hide and seek. It's not enough for me to play it with my friends, so at home, I play it with my little brother. He might be a bit too young for this kind of game, but I've taught him the rules, and he's happy to play it with me. Our apartment is tiny, but thanks to all the clutter, there's enough room for hiding.

Usually, my brother hides first, and I'm the one to search for him. I close my eyes and count to ten while my brother finds a place to hide. It's always the same spot: behind the curtain next to the balcony. But I follow the procedure with all seriousness.

"ARE YOU READY?" I ask in a loud voice after counting to ten, excited to go to the curtain to reveal my brother.

Before I finish the sentence, however, there's a ripple on the curtain and my brother comes out with a beaming smile. "I AM READY!"

My disappointment is huge. I've told him many times not to reveal himself until I find him, but he either forgets or doesn't get the point. So this is how our first round ends every time.

Next, it's my turn to hide. While my brother closes his eyes and counts to ten, I search for the most unexpected place to hide. I climb onto the shelf behind a curtain that separates the kitchen from the living room. Nobody has hidden there before. My heart pumps with a thrill as I hold my breath behind the curtain.

My brother finishes counting and looks for me, but he goes to all the wrong places.

"Where is she?" I hear him ask my parents after a while.

"Oh, where is your sister hiding?"

I stifle a giggle behind the curtain as the silhouettes of my brother and my father pass in front of me. My brother is clearly clueless about my whereabouts. Now what? What will happen next?

A few minutes pass, but nobody comes to find me. As I listen carefully behind the curtain, I hear my brother playing with my father in the back room. I jump off the shelf and storm out from behind the curtain.

"Why aren't you searching for me?" I fume at my brother. "You're supposed to be searching for me!"

"Look, sweetie," my father intervenes gently. "This game is too difficult for him."

I don't say anything. I'm disappointed the game has ended too soon. But because I don't see the point in getting mad, I reluctantly accept the end of our hide and seek, and move on to play something else with my brother.

One day, when I come home after playing with my friends, my mother tells me she's going out for groceries.

"Don't worry, I'll come back soon! But watch over your little brother while I'm away."

"Of course I will!" I answer proudly. I always like being a responsible big sister.

Once my mother is gone, a surge of excitement fills my body. With the absence of adults, my adventurous spirit is called forth. "Let's do something special!"

As I look around, I see my own reflection on the glass door leading to the balcony. Since it's completely dark outside, the glass reflects the entire room like a mirror. I wince and make a pose toward the glass. The girl in the reflection winces back.

I go to the back room, which is connected to the living room with a single sliding door, and from there, I skip toward the glass door, jumping high and making a special pose at the end.

In no time, my little brother joins me. He also skips from the back room toward the glass door and jumps with a wince. One after another, we skip to the glass door, and every time, we make a new pose in the mirror. We even say some fancy words as we jump and make a pose in the air. *We're cool! Look at us! We're amazing!* Each time, we strive to do better than the last time. A higher jump, a bigger smile, a fancier pose, and a cooler message at the end!

As we skip and jump, the tiny living room turns into our universe, and we truly become the coolest kids that have ever existed.

There's a sound of lock turning, and my mother comes back with bags of groceries. My brother and I immediately stop skipping and jumping, and as if nothing happened, we run to welcome our mother. Only the sweat on our bodies and the heated excitement on our faces can tell the amazing place we've just been to while she was away.

One day, I'm alone at home with my brother when he tells me he wants to use the washroom.

"You need to pee?" I ask him like the kindest big sister.

My brother nods and my eyes shine with delight. Nothing excites me more than being a big sister and behaving like one. My little brother needs help, and I'm here to help! Taking my brother's tiny hand, I march through the kitchen to our tiny washroom.

It isn't until we enter the washroom that I realize I've never helped my brother to pee before. I don't even know if he pees the same way as I do. Since I only know of my way of doing it, I decide to go with that.

"Can you stand like this?" I instruct my brother to put one foot on one side of the bowl and the other foot on the other side. Since my brother is still small, I'm afraid he might not be able to hold himself in that position, but with my support, he manages.

Next, I help him to remove his pants, then pee. That part goes smoothly. We're almost done.

Once my brother has finished with peeing, I take some toilet paper and wipe off his peeny. I don't even question it because this is what I normally do for myself. But the moment the toilet paper touches his skin, my brother twists his body, laughing hard as if I tickled his armpits.

What's so funny? Have I done anything wrong? I have no idea. But I'm happy we've successfully completed the mission. I flush the toilet and together we skip back to the back room to resume our play.

Sometime after dinner, my mother prepares futons for all of us in the back room. The room is my brother's and my playroom during the day, but converts into our family's bedroom at night.

In winter, my mother places large thick blankets on top, and when I look at it in the dark, its messy wave reminds me of the ocean. "We're in the middle of an ocean!" I call out to my little brother in the other room, who comes running to see what I'm doing.

There's a small wooden board in our toy collection. It's just a plain wooden board with no particular purpose, but because of that, it can be useful for many things. I grab the board and throw it on top of the blankets. Now it becomes a ship sailing in the sea.

"Look! We're sailing in the ocean. Come on!"

I jump on the board and my brother joins me. The two of us sail in the wavy ocean feeling like the bravest adventurers.

In the tiny kitchen of our apartment, there's a wooden dining table where we eat all our meals and snacks. It's a very basic table: just a plain tabletop supported by four legs.

One day, I'm sitting under the table when I find two dots of white paints on the underside of the tabletop. The dots are blurry on one side, creating tails.

"Shooting stars!" I cry. "We have shooting stars here!"

When my brother joins me under the table, together, we trace the tails with our fingers.

From that day on, watching shooting stars becomes our daily routine. Every evening, after dinner, I say to my brother "Let's go and watch the shooting stars!" and we crawl under the table.

"There goes a shooting star!"

"Oh, another one!"

It's the most predictable, and yet most exciting star gazing. Neither of us has seen a real shooting star before. As I look up at the two shooting stars every night under the kitchen table, I wonder if this is how a real shooting star looks in the real sky.

Mischief

It's dinnertime. We sit around the table in our kitchen; me in front of the fridge, my mother in front of the microwave, and my father in front of the washing machine. My brother is seated between me and my mother, in his high chair with his bib on.

Tonight's dinner is stuffed cabbage rolls served with ketchup. As I stare at the bottle of dark red ketchup on the table, a fun idea strikes me. I take a small amount of ketchup on my forefinger.

"Mommy, look!" I shout as I wave my finger in front of her. "Blood!"

My mother is too busy arranging the food on the table, but my brother notices me. He also wants the ketchup on his finger. So, I drop some on his finger, too.

"Mommy!" We both wave our fingers at our mother. "Blood! Blood!"

"Now, stop that nonsense and eat," says my mother. She doesn't even bother to look at our hands because she knows exactly what we're talking about. No fun. But my brother and I giggle at each other's fake blood.

Next, I start shaking my head. There's no meaning to it, but I'm so full of energy that I cannot sit still. As I shake my head, my hair spreads out, hitting my cheeks.

My brother immediately follows my lead. We both shake our heads faster and faster, laughing at our dancing hair.

"Stop, stop!" Now my father is upset. He's afraid our hair might fly into the food. "You both need to calm down. For goodness' sake, it's dinnertime!"

Finally, my brother and I stop playing. We look at each other and laugh once more before we help ourselves to the food.

One weekend evening after dinner, my mother goes to the sink to wash the dishes, my brother and I go to the living room to play, and my father goes to the washroom.

After a while, I come back to the kitchen looking for my father when I realize he's still in the washroom.

"Daddy, are you pooping?" I shout at the door.

My brother repeats after me, "Are you pooping, Daddy?"

Instead of answering the question, my father tells us to be quiet and go away. This can only mean one thing. He's pooping! My brother and I press on with our next question. "Daddy, when are you coming out?"

In our shabby apartment, there's no such thing as a lock on the washroom door. My brother and I grab the metal doorknob and pull it. The old brown wooden door squeaks and cracks open.

"Stop it!" My father immediately pulls the door from inside, shutting it tight. My brother and I roar with laughter.

"When are you coming out, Daddy?"

We laugh and pull at the door while my father fights hard to keep it shut. Our laughter is now that of madness when my mother finally walks over and intervenes.

"That's enough, sweeties. Leave Daddy alone."

Even amid laughter, I'm quick to notice the serious tone in her voice. Still giggling, I immediately drop my hand, but my brother is still pulling the door.

"Leave him alone," repeats my mother.

Seeing that my brother didn't get her hint, I gently poke him. "Let's go."

We go to the back room to continue our play.

When my father finally comes out of the washroom, exclaiming how naughty we are, my brother and I are already back to our normal selves, the fever of madness gone.

My brother learns to draw with crayons and colour pens. What's particular about his drawings, though, is that he draws the same thing over and over – a round face with many lines sticking out of it. It doesn't look like a human face. When we ask him what he's drawn, his answer is always the same: "A Kind Sun."

One summer day, I'm playing alone in the back room. Sitting in the corner, I doodle in my sketchbook using my new colour pens. It's a hot, sunny day. I lean against the cool white concrete wall when suddenly a wonderful idea occurs to me: this wall would make a perfect canvas!

My mother is busy organizing documents in the next room. She'll likely remain occupied for some time. With a brand-new pink pen in my hand, I call my brother.

"Look here!" I can barely hide my excitement. "Did you know we can draw on the wall – like this?"

I draw a small random pattern on the edge of the largest wall. I know the idea has inspired my brother greatly because the next moment, he's running with his blue pen and drawing an enormous Kind Sun that fills the entire wall.

His bold action impresses me. Up until now, a part of me has wondered if we shouldn't draw on the wall. But all of that is gone after seeing my brother's dynamic drawing. My creativity is unleashed.

We spend a good amount of time filling the white wall with our favourite items in different colours. When we're done, we go to the living room to ask our mother for snacks. She's quick to notice our joyous mood.

"Having a good time?" she smiles at us. "You both look great. Let's have snacks then!"

After our happy snack time, however, my mother needs to grab something from the back room. A heartbeat later, I hear her scream in shock. "What is THIS?"

In that moment, I must have shrunk to the size of a rice grain. I know this voice. We'll be scolded. I turn to my brother, expecting to find a similar reaction, but to my surprise and awe, he's smiling.

"Come here quick!" My mother's angry voice reaches us. "Both of you! NOW!"

When we face her in the back room, she asks us to explain why there are drawings on the wall. Staring at my mother's scary face, I slowly open my mouth. "Well, the white wall was tempting. I tried to draw small ones, but my brother drew this big one."

"It's not a matter of sizes!" she shrieks. "This is a rented apartment, and we must return it at some point! We cannot have this kind of thing on the wall!"

My mother spends the rest of the afternoon scrubbing the wall with a wet towel and soap, but unfortunately, some trace remains. Especially, my brother's Kind Sun is clearly visible even after all the effort of erasing it.

"We'll leave it like this for now," says my mother. "But remember, no more drawing on the wall, please!"

One day, my great-aunt visits us from Tokyo. Since she lives far from us – two hours by bullet train – we don't get to see her often. But she's one of my favourite relatives. She always seems to understand our tender feelings and makes a great playmate. On top of that, like Santa Claus, she never forgets to bring us special gifts that answer our wishes.

We go to the train station to pick her up, and once we get back home, my great-aunt places her bags by the couch and starts chatting with my mother, who is now preparing tea and snacks in the kitchen. My brother and I circle around my great-aunt, wanting to draw her attention but without success.

After a while, I peek into one of her paper bags and jump with delight. There's a box with a Sailor Moon doll I've requested earlier along with a box of toy buses, which has been my brother's request. Now I cannot wait to open my gift. But I need to ask my great-aunt first. I'm not sure how to bring up the topic without sounding greedy, though.

I call my brother to my side. "Can you ask her about the gifts?"

No sooner have I finished my sentence then he runs to my great-aunt, who is still deep in conversation with my mother, and taps on her shoulder. "Where are the gifts?"

No hesitation. No pleasantry. Straight to the point.

My great-aunt turns to my brother and throws her hands into the air in gesture of surprise. "Oh, yes, yes, your gifts!" She picks up the paper bag from the floor. "Here they are! I hope you'll like them!"

My brother and I gather around the bag like squirrels drawn to nuts. We eagerly take out the boxes and open them. The next moment, we're dancing around the room with our dream gifts in our hands.

"My Sailor Moon doll!" I exclaim.

"Look!" My brother waves his new toy buses. "Buses!"

Our heated excitement continues until my mother finally calls all of us for tea and snack.

His Favourites

My two-year-old brother learns how to read, and now he has a few favourite picture books he likes to read out loud. Whenever he's not playing with his toy buses, he goes to the back room of our apartment and pulls out a book from the shelf.

Nontan, Let Me Ride on the Swing! is a book from a series about a mischievous cat named Nontan and his animal friends in the forest. In each story, Nontan does something wrong and learns a lesson through interactions with his friends. In this particular story, Nontan monopolizes the only swing in the playground and upsets his friends.

My brother has read this book so many times that he remembers every line by heart. Yet, whenever he reads out loud, he never forgets to place his finger under each word.

"Nontan, Nontan, let me ride on the swing!" my brother's voice becomes louder as the tension between Nontan and his friends grows. "No, not yet! I'm now going to stand while I ride on the swing!"

His other favourite is a picture book about the famous Winnie the Pooh. It's the story where Pooh visits Rabbit's home, eats too much honey and gets stuck at the entrance on his way out.

My brother has a large Pooh bear plush gifted from a family friend when he was born. Whenever he reads this story, the doll accompanies him to recreate the scene.

"Ei, Ei!" My brother pushes the Pooh bear plush through whatever narrow gap he finds around him. "He wants to go out, but he ate too much. He's stuck!"

I don't know what about these two stories appeal to him so much. But my brother never seems to get bored of them, and now the stories start running in my head, too.

Weekday

It's a weekday morning. I never seem to notice the morning's arrival until my mother comes to wake me up.

"Sweetie!" she calls out in a loud voice that yanks me out of sleep. "Time to wake up!"

In our tiny living room, my little brother is already up, toddling around the small low table carrying the bowls of yogurt and spoons for both of us, being a big boy. Meanwhile, I drag myself across the room to change into my daywear with my eyes still half-closed.

"Be quick," says my mother from the kitchen. "We'll be leaving soon!"

There's usually less than half an hour before I leave home for kindergarten. I sit at the low table next to my brother and eat fruit and yogurt. The TV is on in the background to keep track of time.

At some point, my mother calls me to the kitchen to tie my hair for the day.

"One, two, or half-up?" she asks me, holding a comb and hair ties. One means a ponytail, two means pigtails, and half-up means the most basic half-up hair.

Once that's done and I finish my breakfast, it's time for us to leave home.

"Come quick!" says my mother again as I collect my yellow bag and yellow hat and walk to the door in a sluggish movement. "Say bye to your brother!"

My brother usually stays at home for the next fifteen minutes or so while my mother takes me to kindergarten. It's fine because my father is technically at home, albeit asleep.

"Bye!" I wave at my brother. "See you later!"

And off we go. Down the staircase into the fresh morning air. A new day is beginning.

In the afternoon, when I come home from kindergarten, my mother, brother and I sit for our teatime. My mother starts the kettle and takes out a box of McVitie's chocolate biscuits from the shelf while my brother and I hold our plastic plates tightly in anticipation.

At my home, there are two kinds of snacks kept on the shelf: McVitie's chocolate biscuits, and a mix of spicy rice crackers and peanuts. Because my mother doesn't approve of potato chips and other popular snacks I enjoy eating at my friends' places, these two are the only options at home. They both make an appearance once a day, and that's when we have our afternoon teatime.

Once my mother finishes pouring the hot tea into three cups, my attention goes to the box of McVitie's biscuits. She sets two biscuits on each plate before putting away the box.

"You'll have them again tomorrow," says my mother reassuringly, as if answering my lingering gaze on the box.

Once the box is gone, my eager gaze drops to the two round biscuits on my plate. A smile of satisfaction spreads on my face. These are mine!

Wanting to indulge in the excitement a little longer, I shift my attention to my plate. The plastic plate has a wide rim which has illustrations of many different snack items: candies, donuts, biscuits, ice cream. I point at them one by one as I sing a song everyone knows at my kindergarten: "Which one shall I choose? Let the fate decide!"

My brother's plate doesn't have many illustrations, but he tries to follow along with me, pointing at a few illustrations on his plate and singing the song.

Next, I turn my attention to the biscuits. I place one on top of the other so that they look like a snowman.

"Oh, look!" I exclaim as if making a new discovery, even though I've done it countless times. "A snowman is here! Snowman, snowman, snowman!"

My brother is quick to follow me. Placing one biscuit on top of the other, he joins the chorus. "Snowman, snowman, snowman!"

By the time we finish playing, my mother's plate is empty. We spend the next few minutes eating biscuits and sipping tea in peace.

When teatime is over, my mother guides us into two different activities: a nap for my brother, and a study session for me. Neither of us is thrilled, but for me, the next one hour is the darkest time of my day. My mother has a math workbook to teach me basic arithmetic and geometry, and every day, she picks a few questions for me to work on. I'm not allowed to go out to play with my friends until I'm done with the questions.

After clearing the table for my study session, my mother takes out a package of spicy rice crackers and peanuts and pours them into a small bowl, circles a few questions in my math workbook, then walks over to the back room to put down my brother for his nap.

As I sip the remaining milk tea and read the questions, my face becomes gloomy. I have no idea how I'm going to spend the next hour with these dry, tasteless problems, which I'm clueless how to solve. All I want is to play with my friends. I am already brainstorming what fun things we'll do today once I'm free.

I throw a few spicy rice crackers into my mouth and read the questions again. I try scribbling something in my notebook, hoping to look like I'm thinking. I'd rather solve these questions for real, but sadly, I'm hopeless when it comes to math questions. So, I do the next best thing: I pretend.

This is a tricky game. My mother is short-tempered when supervising my study session. She doesn't like to see me stuck in a question she believes she's already taught me how to solve.

"You stupid!" she often explodes at me. "Why can't you even solve this *easy* question?"

One day, my mother and I get into a bad fight before my brother falls asleep. My eyes are already puffy from crying as she goes to my brother in the back room to help him sleep.

One thing we forgot to consider is that there's not much distance between where I'm studying and where my brother is laid. He's heard all our unkind words, and these days, he has a habit of repeating what others have said.

Just when my mother puts a blanket on him, my brother opens his mouth.

"She's stupid," his innocent voice echoes in the room. "Am I a good boy?"

The timing couldn't have been worse.

"SHUT UP!" I explode at my brother across the room, my face covered with tears, my nose runny, and my voice hoarse from shouting. I really don't need to be called stupid by my little brother.

Thankfully, though I'm not sure how, the battle between me and my mother calms down after that. I somehow finish my work in an hour, and I'm heading out to play with my friends with a smile on my face, relieved to be released from the poisonous study session for now.

One afternoon, I'm yet again having a tantrum over my daily quota of math questions. I haven't been making a good progress, and my mother becomes snappy. I feel gloomy at the prospect of another fight after having come out of a particularly intense one only recently.

Just when the tension between us has heightened to a dangerous degree, a bright light flashes across the sky and thunder roars. As I look outside, there's another lightning flash followed by a loud noise, and it starts pouring. *Just like our fight.* With a heavy sigh, I force my eyes back to my math question, trying my best to look like I'm thinking hard.

To my surprise, however, my mother's not paying attention to me. She walks over to the glass door leading to our tiny balcony.

"This is quite a sight." She sounds impressed as she looks up at the dark sky. She turns in my direction. "Come, sweetie." Her voice is kind. "How about you sit here and we'll watch the thunderstorm together?"

I'd do anything to be free from my boring task. I happily sit next to my mother in front of the open balcony door. Shoulder to shoulder, we watch the dramatic lightning show in the sky without words. Simply mesmerized by the sight and the sound.

As the brief storm comes to an end and sunlight peeks through the thick clouds, my mother puts an arm around my shoulder and says to me, "That was fun, wasn't it?"

I'm so taken aback by the delight in my mother's voice that I don't speak for a second. But then, excitement replaces my surprise. I grin at her. "Yes, that was really fun!"

We both slowly go back to the kitchen table to resume my math study. My workbook remains open at the page where I was struggling. But now, the air is light. There's no more shouting or screaming. In no time, I finish my daily quota and go out to play with my friends under the now clear sky.

When I come home after playing with my friends, there's usually some time before supper. I sit in front of the TV with my back leaned against the brown wooden cupboard. My brother quickly joins me, and together we watch the late afternoon programs for kids.

The first one to come on the screen is "With Mommy!" an educational program designed for toddlers. Though I've officially outgrown it, I still like watching it. The main characters are two dogs, a sister and a brother, just like us. The sister dog loves playing soccer, but her brother and friends are always afraid of her powerful shots. This routine is the part my brother and I enjoy most. Whenever the sister picks up the ball, we laugh in anticipation.

Then we watch an English educational program titled "Play in English!" A Japanese girl named Miku and an elder gentleman, Uncle Jerry, teach us some easy English phrases while going through their daily routines. My brother loves Uncle Jerry and his obsession with stylish hats. Each episode ends with Uncle Jerry getting a new hat to add to his large hat collection and Miku disapproving of his secret purchase. My brother and I laugh at our favourite scene.

Around this time, my mother often calls out to see if we want to try some food she's preparing. My brother jumps to his feet and runs to the kitchen, where my mother puts a piece of cooked vegetables in his mouth.

Finally, my favourite program arrives – a short anime about three ninja boys. The series is designed for older kids and has a more complex storyline, making it less interesting for my brother.

When this program is over, my mother calls us for supper. Our TV time is over for today.

After dinner, while my mother cleans up the kitchen, I practice the piano. My brother goes to play on his own, but my mother calls him back to the kitchen. It's his daily medication time. My brother runs to where my mother holds out a spoonful of medication, opens his mouth and swallows the content before running back to the living room.

Soon, my practice is over, and my brother and I play together until my mother calls both of us for our bath time.

On weekday evenings, my mother, brother, and I take a bath together. My mother first washes me while my brother waits for his turn on the small chair in the corner.

Our apartment is very old, and so, different kinds of bugs make appearances every now and then. There's one pill bug that lives in the bathroom and often emerges from the water pipe when we take a bath, next to the spot where my brother's sitting.

"There goes a pill bug!" I shout, pointing at the dark spot moving toward my brother's feet. "Over there!"

My brother panics, trying to move away from the bug, but my mother stops him.

"Calm down." She gives us both a stern look. She never appreciates disruptions to the task at hand – in this case, taking a bath. "It's just a bug. No need to make a fuss about it!"

After my mother washes me and my brother, the two of us sit in the bathtub by ourselves while my mother showers in the washing area.

This is a golden moment, a moment when we can play and splash as much water as we want. Once my mother joins us, she'll make us sit quietly, but now, we're free to do whatever we like.

I pick up toys in both hands – a bucket, a watering can, and a few empty toy capsules – and march in the bathtub.

"Anything, everything, tick, tick, tick!" I sing as I walk around.

My brother immediately follows my lead. Picking up toys in his hands, he walks behind me.

"Anything, everything, tick, tick, tick!"

We sing together as we go round and round in the bathtub, our voices becoming louder and our movements bigger. Just when our fun has reached its climax, my mother finishes her washing and joins us in the bathtub.

"Sweeties, that's it!" My mother's calm voice echoes in the heated bathroom. "We're now going to sit and warm up properly."

One evening, the three of us are relaxed in the bathtub when my mother suddenly turns to my brother in her lap. "You've just peed, sweetie, haven't you?"

I've been happily playing with the water, but my body stills upon hearing the unsettling comment.

"Did you really pee?" I turn to my brother. "Did you?"

My brother doesn't answer, but his innocent smile confirms my suspicion.

"You *peed* in the bath!"

I cannot believe it. All the water is now contaminated by my brother's pee.

"I'm out of here!" I wrestle to get out of the bath, but my mother grabs my shoulder and pushes me back into the water. Mercilessly. "Warm up properly."

To my horror, I'm forced to immerse myself all the way up to my shoulders. With or without pee in the bath, my mother is determined to complete our bath time without disruption.

"I can't believe you peed in the bath!" I repeat over and over as I glare at my smiley brother.

When my mother finally releases me, I shoot out of the bathtub like a rocket, out of contamination.

These days, my mother's mildly troubled by the tightness in her back muscles. Instead of searching for a massage therapist nearby, she suggests a new evening activity for me and my brother. After dinner and bath, my mother goes to the back room and lies on her stomach. "Sweeties, you can play on my back!"

This is such a fun invitation from our mother, who's strict with us during the day. Jumping with delight, my brother and I climb onto her back. After some exploration, we each find our favourite spot.

My brother likes to stand on our mother's back, then pretending he's lost balance, fall on the floor, screaming "Oh, noooooo!"

Meanwhile, I sit between my mother's legs in the back. Her legs are moving idly, but suddenly, they both fly to me and sandwich me. "Help!" I scream. "A monster is trying to eat me!"

We both repeat this forever – my brother falling from our mother's back and me screaming between her moving legs.

Finally, my mother tells us to stop. "Thanks, sweeties," she says, sitting up. "Oh, I feel *much* better. This is it for tonight!"

"Already?" My brother and I protest. "We want to do more!"

"That's it for tonight," she repeats as she stands up. "But we can do it again tomorrow!"

From that day on, "playing on Mommy's back" becomes our favourite evening activity.

Before going to bed, my mother, brother, and I have a short reading time. Dressed in pajamas, we huddle on the family couch in the living room. In front of us, my mother spreads the collection of books and picture story shows – *kamishibai* in Japanese – that we borrowed from the library last weekend.

"Which one do we read tonight?"

Some nights, my brother and I choose a picture book from one of our favourite series: the Nontan series, the adventures of eleven cats or of ten frogs. We sit on either side of our mother, and as she reads the story aloud, we point at the funny details of the picture and ask why the story is unfolding in the way it is.

Other nights, my mother reads us a picture story show. She sits on the couch holding up a pile of large picture boards in her hands while my brother and I sit on the floor looking up at the picture like in a theatre.

Once my mother starts reading the story from behind the picture, our excitement explodes. My brother says something about the picture, I add my own comment, my brother says something else, and so on. We're nonstop chatting, and my mother has to intervene to make us quiet so that she can carry on with the story.

When the story comes to an end, two words appear on the last picture board in bold lettering: THE END. No sooner than the words appear, my brother jumps to his feet and rushes to the final page our mother is holding.

"THE. END." He points his finger at each word as he slowly and deliberately pronounces the two words.

"That's right, sweetie," my mother smiles. "It says 'The End'! Good job!"

My brother's face glows with pride.

When the reading is over, it's time for me and my brother to go to bed. But there's one more fun activity before sleeping. It's a game my mother has devised, called Whee! where my mother carries each of us to our futons in the back room and releases us with a loud "Whee!"

My brother and I love this game. As soon as my mother asks us "Who wants to play Whee!?" we become enthusiastic, forgetting it'll lead us to bed.

My brother is always the first to go. I wait in the living room while my mother carries him to the back room and releases him with a big "Whee!" When she comes back to pick me up, I have a special request ready. "I want to do Wooo!"

Wooo! is exactly the same as Whee! except that at the end my mother releases me with a big "Wooo!" But to my toddler brother, it counts as another game. The moment I land next to my brother with my mother's big "Wooo!" he rises to his feet. "Me too, me too. I want to do Wooo!"

It gives me a sense of satisfaction to see my little brother being jealous of me. He keeps asking our mother for Wooo! but the game is over for tonight, and he'll have to wait until tomorrow night.

But then things take an unexpected turn. After a few unsuccessful attempts to distract him, my mother gives in to my brother's request, carrying him back to the living room to do Wooo!

The moment my brother lands next to me with my mother's big "Wooo!" I rise to my feet. "I want to do it again, too!"

"No, sweetie." My mother gives me a stern look. "We're done for tonight."

"That's not fair!" I'm now upset. "He did it twice! I also want to do Wooo! again!"

But she doesn't accept my request. She tells me to wait until tomorrow and leaves the room.

Weekend

It's a weekend morning. As soon as my eyes open, I locate my mother. Being an early riser, her sleeping spot on my left is always empty by the time I wake up.

In our tiny apartment, you can hear any sound coming from any room. All I need to do is to listen carefully. My mother's usually in the living room, working on her enormous typewriter. Sure enough, her typing sound reaches my ears, followed by a peaceful pause when she's most likely taking a sip of her morning coffee.

I roll out of my blanket and walk over to the living room, rubbing my sleepy eyes.

"Good morning, sweetie!" My mother is quick to notice me. "Did you sleep well?"

Just as I've pictured, she's sitting in front of her typewriter with a cup of coffee in her hand.

Instead of answering her question, I walk straight to her lap and seat myself on one half. There was once a time when I used to occupy all of her lap, but now, I leave one half for my little brother, who can be up at any moment.

I love this morning cuddle time when my mother's still in her fresh, happy mood. At this hour, she's nothing but sweet and kind. Staring at the stitches on her pajamas, I remain quiet for some time. We then talk about this and that, nothing too important, just a pleasant exchange of words.

After some time, a figure appears at the sliding door separating the living room from the backroom. My brother stands there, his eyes half-closed and his short hair messy from sleep.

"Good morning!" My mother and I greet him at the same time. "Did you sleep well?"

Nodding without words, my brother comes straight to the other half of our mother's lap, the one I've kept for him. Now, her lap is fully occupied. And we all chat about this and that – a meaningless but pleasant exchange of words – until finally, my mother decides it's time for us to get changed and have breakfast.

One weekend morning when I wake up, both my mother's and brother's sleeping spots are empty. They're having a morning cuddle time in the next room. Their quiet voices drift through the open sliding door.

As I become fully awake, I suddenly remember I left my dolls in the middle of a dramatic love story last night. Now is a perfect moment to continue that story because I won't be disturbed!

Smiling, I reach for my toy box at my feet where I keep my dolls, careful not to make any sound. But the tin box is empty. That's when I realize all my dolls are under the digital piano in the living room where I left them last night. I was too lazy to put them back in the box.

"Bummer!"

I crawl back to my blanket and lie down, thinking hard what to do. If I stay here, my mother will think I'm still asleep and I won't be disturbed. But without my dolls, what's the point?

If I go to pick up my dolls, however, she'll probably tell me to get changed and have breakfast. I don't want that yet. I stare at the ceiling, torn.

Finally, my desire to play with the dolls wins. I run to the living room, grab my dolls from under the piano, then dash back to the back room. On the way, I catch a glimpse of my mother and brother staring at me with surprise.

"Oh?" I hear my brother's amused voice as I slip back under my blanket with the dolls. "*Oh*?"

"That was your sister," comes my mother's voice. "She was in a great hurry, wasn't she?"

They're now talking about me, but I couldn't care less. I'm already immersed in the love story of my dolls.

Sadly, though, my happy time is short-lived. A few minutes later, my mother walks in and lifts my blanket from my face. "Aren't you getting up, sweetie? I know you're awake!"

"No, I'm not!" I reply, my eyes shut. "The person you saw just now wasn't me! That was somebody else!"

Laughing, she tells me to get changed so that we can eat breakfast. With a sigh of disappointment, I reluctantly crawl out of my blanket to start my day.

Some time after breakfast, while my father's still asleep in the back room, my mother takes me and my brother out to the public art gallery near our home. Our interest isn't the exhibitions, but the great picnic spots outside the gallery.

With a bag full of snacks, the three of us leave home on foot. We walk out the gate of our community of apartments, travel through another community of equally old, but larger apartments, and down the hill until finally a familiar brown concrete building appears in front of us.

The art gallery has a spacious garden, called the Garden of Alice, its design inspired by Lewis Carroll's famous book *Alice in Wonderland*. Once we arrive, we head for this garden first. We pass through the main hallway and exit the back door into the courtyard.

I bounce with excitement as we come to my favourite part – the rabbit hole. The garden passage starts with a vertical tunnel that reminds me of the rabbit hole of *Alice in Wonderland*. In my head, I pretend we've just fallen down the hole and entered a magical world like in the story.

The garden is indeed magical. A passage leads us through different statues, which we can touch or in some cases even ride, like the large metal cheshire cat in front of a wall of mirrors. After riding on the cat, my brother and I run along the mirrors.

"Yahoo!" I call out, my voice coming back in echoes.

"Yahoo!" My brother's voice joins the chorus.

The magical passage eventually gives way to a little park. We pick a place to sit, and my mother opens our snack bag. Grabbing a few snacks in our hands – among them our favourite Muscat grape chewing gum – my brother and I run to the little pond at the centre of the park where large carp swim under the water. We lean against the bar, putting snacks in our mouths and watching the fish move around below us.

Just when we're immersed in the magical world, our mother calls us. The three of us then walk back to the building, back to the ordinary world.

Sometimes in the afternoon we go to the public library near our home. This time, my father also joins us.

The library is only a few minutes drive from home. We pass the post office and the art gallery, then cross a bridge toward the city centre. Half-hidden in the woods on the riverside is the small one-story building of our library, just as old and neglected as our home.

Once inside, my father goes to the right, heading to the adults' book section, and the rest of us turn left, toward the children's book section. I then leave my mother and brother to begin my own exploration.

There's a bookshelf by the window that carries many storybooks. Their stories are longer than picture books, perfect for someone like me who's no longer a beginning reader.

The series I'm into at the moment is *Thomas the Tank Engine*. Earlier, I used to read their picture book series, but now I've switched to their storybook series. They have more words and fewer illustrations – meaning more interesting details are described in words!

While I stand by the window, absorbed in the book, my mother and brother choose a few picture story shows and several picture books. Some for our bedtime reading and others for my brother. After a while, they come to find me.

"Sweetie," my mother calls out, extending her arms to collect my books. "While I check these out, can you go and find Daddy, please?"

This week's library visit is coming to an end. I dash to the other side of the library, from the noisy side to the quieter, more serious part of the building. The bookshelves tower over me, and the smell of old books tickles my nose. Before long, I spot a familiar figure between the shelves.

"Daddy!" I almost shout, forgetting that this is a serious section of the library. "Mommy said we're going home!"

In the brief moment before my father collects all his books, I pick up a random book from the shelf and flip through the pages. Even though I've become good at reading, this is something else.

Words are dense on each page, and not even a single picture can be found.

"So, Daddy, *who* reads this book?" I ask my father, frowning. "Is this really fun to read?"

A laugh is the only response I get from my father as he tells me to put the book back on the shelf and leaves for the checkout counter with his pile of books.

As I follow him back to the centre of the building – to the place between the noisy section and the serious section of the library – a sense of wonder fills my heart. I don't think I'll ever read those dense, pictureless books. Still, knowing that a whole new world exists outside of my familiar one appeals to my adventurous spirit, and I like that.

Some Sundays, my family drives to a large shopping mall on the outskirts of our town to buy things we cannot find in the neighbourhood stores. I always look forward to the drive because it's long enough to enjoy the scenery and the music from the car audio – the song cassettes my father has made for us.

I usually sit on the right side of the back seat while my brother sits on the left. The excitement of going on a long drive makes both of us talk in loud voices, sometimes so loud that my parents think we're fighting.

On the way, we drive across a little hilltop. Among the stores and houses stands a gigantic stone figure. It's a statue of the Goddess of Mercy built by the owner of a hotel nearby. My parents say they built it to show off their wealth, but what interests me and my brother more is the statue's funny face.

The moment the massive white stone figure comes into sight, my brother and I stop whatever we're doing and look out of the window.

"Is that a *strange* woman?" I say, turning to my brother.

"Is that a *strange* man?" says my brother.

Then we burst into laughter.

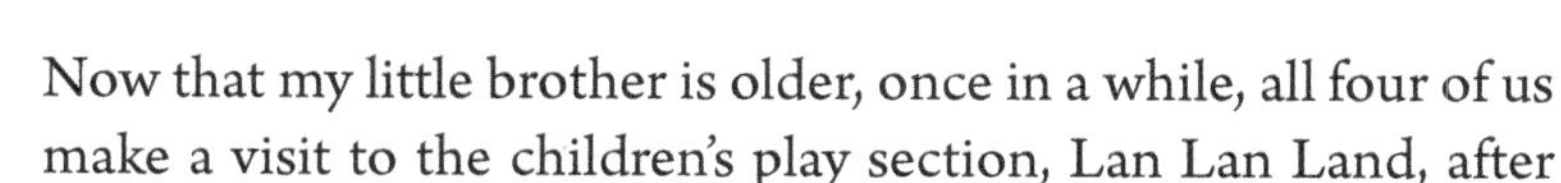

Now that my little brother is older, once in a while, all four of us make a visit to the children's play section, Lan Lan Land, after shopping.

First we do what all the visitors do: visit the attractions. My mother, brother and I take a ride on the toy train that looks like Thomas from the famous TV series *Thomas and Friends*. The small train goes around half the floor of the play space. There are artificial stations, mountains, and towns along the track, and I pretend we're travelling on a real locomotive.

We also try the merry-go-round. It's a smaller version of what I saw in an amusement park, but it's fun to ride on the fake horses with my mother and brother, going round and round until the music stops. As the familiar scenery swirls around me, I pretend we're riding real horses in a real field.

Once we're done with the main attractions, my brother and I are free to play on our own. I take my brother to some of my favourite spots. Our first stop is a group of large fake houses. I go to one of them, telling my brother that I live there. "Which one is *your* house?"

My brother picks the one next to mine, and we take turns in being a guest in each other's house until my brother becomes interested in something else: a large fake tree at the centre of the play section.

"Come, there's a special hiding spot!"

I lead my brother to the bottom of the tree where a large hole opens up so that children can go inside. I crawl into the tree, followed by my brother. He likes the place so much that once inside, he doesn't want to come out. Even after I leave, he stays there with his smiley face, looking to surprise our mother and father through the hole.

Another Sunday, we've just finished shopping at the mall and are driving back home. My father sits in the back seat between me and my brother to keep the peace between us while my mother focuses on driving. Now that we're tired from the day, my brother and I can easily get into fights.

Today, however, my father takes out something from his little shopping bag. It's a metal toy bus modelled after a yellow kindergarten bus. Earlier, while my father and I roamed around the mall together, he purchased it as a surprise souvenir for my brother, who was accompanying my mother for the household shopping.

"But he doesn't like kindergarten buses," I said to my father. "He only likes city buses, remember?"

Though my brother is a lover of buses and a collector of toy buses, he only likes large city buses and shows no interest in small private ones, like shuttle buses and kindergarten buses. To him, they're not *real* buses.

"Don't be so picky," my father said to me as he placed the yellow kindergarten bus in his shopping basket. "It's still a bus, and your brother will like it!"

Now my father shows the yellow toy bus to my brother in the back seat of the car. "Surprise, surprise! I've got a bus for you, sweetie! Do you want it?"

It's dark, and we can barely see anything properly. But my brother is immediately interested. He takes the metal toy bus in his hand and eagerly studies what kind of bus he's got, which makes my father happy. But I cannot stop myself from revealing the truth.

"It's not a real bus, though," I say to my brother. "It's a kindergarten bus!"

"Shhhh!" My father frowns at me. "You don't have to tell him that! He cannot tell!"

"But it's a kindergarten bus!" I repeat to my brother, laughing.

He spends the rest of the journey playing with the bus. But as soon as we get back home and turn the light on, he realizes that it's a yellow kindergarten bus. My brother puts the bus at the far end of his toy bus collection and moves on to do something else.

My father blames me for my brother's lost interest in the new toy bus, but I cannot stop laughing. I cannot believe he underestimated my brother's taste for buses and bought him a kindergarten bus in the first place.

On weekend nights, my father reads me a bedtime story. He's now reading *The Hobbit*. It's the thickest book he's ever read me, and I greatly admire the beauty of this book – its blue cover, the fresh fragrance of the smooth paper inside, and the ribbon bookmark.

Before reading, my father makes a cup of hot green tea for himself and brings it to the bedside. It's his habit to drink tea while reading to me.

In the next room, my mother reads a picture book to my little brother. He's still too young to join my father's bedside reading, so he has his own reading time with our mother.

One night, my brother finishes early and comes to join us. He crawls to the other side of our father and lies down. In our miniscule apartment, the space is always tight. Just when my father finishes reading and puts down the book, my brother moves and knocks over my father's now cold green tea. The tea spills over *The Hobbit* and onto the floor.

"Oh, no!" My father quickly grabs tissue paper and wipes off the water from the book. But it's too late. There's now a huge dark stain across the beautiful blue cover and the pages are wavy.

And my eyes widen with surprise. One moment, my father announced the end of tonight's story, and the next, he was running for a tissue to save the book from the spilled tea.

My brother isn't aware of the damage he's caused to the book, but the stain on the blue cover will always be a reminder of this night's event.

The Summer

One summer day, my family visits a local aquarium. I've been there a few times already, but it's the first visit for my brother.

At the aquarium, we split into two teams – me and my mother on one team, and my brother and father on the other – so as to accommodate our age gap and different interests.

After the day's outing, on our way back home, my father shares a funny story about when he took my brother to a sea lion show. As the two of them sat in the back, watching several sea lions play tricks in front of the audience, my brother opened his mouth.

"A mouse!" he said, pointing to the sea lions.

"A mouse?" My father was puzzled for a second. But then it struck him that from where they sat, the sea lions looked much smaller than their actual size, and with the long whiskers, they must have reminded my brother of a mouse he'd seen in his picture books.

"A mouse!" said my brother again.

"Sweetie, that's not a mouse," my father gently corrected him. "That's a sea lion."

"That's not a mouse, that's a sea lion."

"That's right. That's a sea lion."

With his eyes glued to the sea lions on the stage, my brother repeated what he'd just learned once again. "That's not a mouse, that's a sea lion!"

Both my mother and I laugh upon hearing the story, since it's typical of my brother to repeat his new knowledge over and over. The story becomes one of my family's favourites.

Another day, my family visits a local indoor water park. It's my first time to play in a large indoor pool, and I'm amazed to find multiple spacious pools in one big room. There's also a big slide towering over us.

My mother hands me and my brother swim rings so that we can play in the water. Neither of my parents can swim well, so they have no intention of teaching us. We're left to play in the water as we wish.

I lie on top of my big swim ring, making myself comfortable. From this angle, the whole room looks different. I spend a long time floating in the water like that, enjoying the way the water caresses my back.

I'm completely absorbed in my own world when my father asks me if I want to try the waterslide.

"Waterslide?" I sit up on my swim ring and ask my father what it is. I've never heard of such a thing before. My father points to the large, colorful slide I saw upon entering the room. It has a lot of turns and twirls. Looks like fun. I decide to give it a try.

We walk to the staircase leading up to the slide and wait in the queue. As my turn comes closer, my father leaves me, telling me he'll wait at the end of the slide to see me come out.

When my turn finally arrives, I sit on the shiny red surface. This slide is a tube, and unlike the slide on a playground, I cannot see where it's leading. Somebody's voice calls out from behind me. "You have to push forward!"

That's the last thing I hear as I give a push and my body launches forward.

The slide is very slippery. The moment my body starts descending, there's no place I can hold onto. I'm carried along the tube downward at an increasing speed, making turns here and there. I cannot see where I'm going, and my eyes are fixed on the red slippery wall around me.

Just when I relax and think to myself how amazing it is that this slide is like a tunnel, a blue opening suddenly appears in front of me. For a split second, I wonder what it is. And then –

Splash! I drop into the water, and I'm in over my head. I didn't even get the chance to control my breathing, and I've gulped a huge amount of chlorine water. A sharp pain explodes in my nose. Panicking and gagging, I fight to get my face above the water.

When I finally get to my feet, I'm angry and crying. Such a horror awaited at the end of this water slide! Why didn't anyone warn me about it?

I find my father laughing to tears as he comes to pick me up. He says it was funny when I came out of the hole and immediately dropped into the water. We go back to join my mother and brother in the peaceful shallow pool. I tell them what happened, and my mother also laughs. But I'm not laughing. As I climb back on my swim ring, I'm still upset about the chlorine water that filled my mouth and nose. I swear I'll never try a waterslide ever again.

Sometime in August, I visit my maternal grandmother's house with my mother and brother. One hot day during our stay, my mother says we can play in the bathtub.

"There's lukewarm water in the bathtub from last night," she tells us. "You two can play in the water. It'll be cool and nice!"

Unlike our bathtub back home, the one at my grandmother's house is huge. There's even room to walk around. My brother and I are balls of excitement as we remove our clothes and climb into the water with toys in our hands. After seeing that we're good on our own, my mother leaves us to attend to other tasks.

My brother and I play our usual game. We circle around inside the bathtub, shaking toys in our hands.

"Anything, everything, tick, tick, tick!" we chant, our voices and movements growing bigger with each step we take.

Suddenly, amid our dance, my brother slips and falls under the water. At first, I don't think much of it. He's tall enough to get out. But the shock of falling has panicked him. He's gagging under the water, making no attempt to stand up.

I quickly grab my brother's arm and pull him up. His face comes above the water for a second, but he's panicking so much that he slips and falls back into the water again. He's crying. I can see his red and wrinkled face, but his voice is blocked by the water. I pull him up again, this time harder, making sure his feet won't slip.

As soon as his face comes out of the water, my brother's powerful cry pierces the air, echoing and filling the bathroom. I hear a quick footstep in the corridor, and the next second, my mother appears at the door.

"What happened?" she asks, her eyes scanning the bathroom.

I explain that my brother has slipped and fallen in the water. "I pulled him up from the water, and he's okay now. But he won't stop crying."

My mother immediately takes my brother out of the water and carries him away to calm him down.

As I sit in the water, listening to the fading cry of my brother in the corridor, I feel the magic disappear. Just a moment ago, we were playing and dancing happily. But the party is over now. My heart sinks in disappointment before I finally stand up and get out of the water.

Shortly after we return home, the news of a small *Bon Odori* festival in our neighbourhood reaches us. It's hosted in a park near the local Shinto shrine where we did the *Mikoshi* festival earlier this year. Recalling the fun memories of the *Bon Odori* festival I experienced at my grandmother's place, I tell my mother I want to go.

The evening of the festival, my mother takes me and my little brother to the park. It's our first time to participate in our community's *Bon Odori* festival, since we're usually at my grandmother's place this time of August.

In the middle of the park is a pop-up tower, just like I remember from the festival at my grandmother's place. Inside the tower, the singer and drummers are playing music. It's already been some time since the festival started, and people are dancing around the tower in a circle. I dash to the circle, excited to join the dance while my mother and brother follow me on the side.

Ten seconds into the dance, however, my mood is no longer merry. I don't know the steps. The music and the dance of this *Bon Odori* are different from those at my grandmother's place. I try to mimic the movements of those around me, but it's too fast for me to follow. Soon, I'm in tears.

"I can't do it! I can't do it!" I stomp in frustration. This is my typical expression of panic and stress, and my mother hates seeing it.

"Don't stress, sweetie, just follow others!"

"I can't do it! I can't do it! They're too fast!" I cry, stomping again.

My mother tries to cheer me up, but after a few unsuccessful attempts, she loses her temper. "We came here to enjoy the festival. If you keep whining like that, we're going home!"

This only makes me cry louder. "No, I'm not going home! I want to dance!"

"Then do it without whining!"

"But they're too fast!" I cry. "I can't follow the steps!"

Just when my mother reaches for my hand to grab me out of the circle, an older lady appears in front of us. She's dressed in a traditional costume. "Look at me," she says, spreading her arms in preparation for the dance. "I'll do the moves slowly. So, follow me."

She dances to the music with slower and bigger movements, and I follow behind her, copying every move she makes. The lady watches me carefully, nods if I do it right and shows me the move again if I don't get it.

I'm no longer crying. All my attention is now focused on the lady's movements. With an empty mind, I follow her again and again while my mother and brother silently follow us on the side.

After a few rounds, I finally memorize all the steps and can now dance in time with everybody else around me. It feels wonderful. Seeing that I'm fine on my own, the lady leaves us, congratulating me on my accomplishment and wishing me good luck. My mother thanks her with a deep bow.

Tonight, I have great fun dancing around with other people. On our way home, I cannot stop telling my mother how well I've danced and how happy I am. My face glows with pride, as if my earlier whining and stomping never happened.

My mother listens quietly, holding my brother's hand in one hand and mine in the other.

Sometime during the summer, a rumour arrives that the International Tchaikovsky Competition for Young Musicians will be held in our town this year.

I'm no aspiring musician, but since the competition is so famous and it's such a rare opportunity for us to listen to talented young musicians, my mother and my two best friends' mothers decide to take us three girls to the competition for one day. An educational outing, so to speak.

There's just one problem, though. Because this is a serious competition, only children over six years old who are capable of remaining quiet during the performance can sit in the audience.

Luckily, my friends and I are all tall for our age. It's decided that we'll pretend to be six years old. As for our little siblings, there's no way they can be quiet, so they'll stay at home with their fathers.

"Be very quiet!" A deadly serious warning is given to us before we enter the concert hall. "No chatting, no laughing. Understood?"

The fact that we have to pretend to be older makes me feel excited about this adventure. I march into the large hall with Sakura and Karen, wondering what amazing performances we'll get to see on the stage.

Once the competition begins, however, it's like any other piano concert. Young adult performers come out on stage one by one, and they perform rather long piano pieces. I'm quickly bored, but remembering the solemn oath I took earlier, I remain still and silent, observing the gorgeous dresses of the female participants and counting the number of spotlights on the ceiling. I'm eager to leave this stifling dark place and play with my friends outside.

Later that day, when we're back home, my father tells us about the most "awful" day he's had with my brother.

While we were away, my father took my brother on a subway ride, then to a shopping mall to entertain him. After a successful outing, on their way home, my father went to use a public washroom at a subway station. Once he'd taken care of both of their needs in a booth, he flushed the toilet as he'd normally do.

The next moment, however, water began to rise in the toilet bowl. It kept rising, carrying things he didn't want to see or even think about. My father ran, with my brother in his arms, out of the booth, out of the washroom, away from the approaching disaster! All the while, my brother remained calm because he didn't understand what was happening.

"It was the worst day ever!" my father concludes while my mother and I burst into laughter. "We faced such a disaster while you folks indulged in high culture!"

Contrary to my father's comment, I'm now full of envy. Who knew such a fun adventure was taking place while I endured my educational outing? I wish I'd gone with them.

Yamaha Music School and Sibling Privilege

Once every week, I go to a group lesson at the local Yamaha music school with Sakura and Karen. Once we park the car inside the shopping arcade, the nine of us walk over to the music shop.

In front of the building, there's a large mechanical clock hanging from the arcade's ceiling. A quiet anticipation builds in the air as we come to a halt and look up. That's when the clock strikes the hour and its golden doors swing open. The famous "Canon" by Pachelbel plays from above us while dolls dressed in old foreign clothes appear and nod their heads to the music. The figures in the centre look like a king and queen.

For a moment, we all forget why we're here. With our gaze fixed on the moving figures under the clock, we're caught by their magic. From the corner of my eye, I see my little brother nodding his head with the dolls.

Then, just as suddenly as it started, the music stops and the dolls retreat behind the closing doors. Time flows again, and our mothers usher us into the building. Our class is starting soon.

"When will the dolls come out again?" somebody asks.

"We'll meet them again next week!" my mother says. "We say goodbye for now!"

And that's our weekly ritual – to be enchanted by the magic of the mechanical clock before running to our class.

There's one song my little brother loves singing these days: "It's a Small World After All." The song is in the textbook I use for my music lessons. The book comes with a CD with all the songs played by professional musicians, which my mother often plays in the evening.

Even though I'm the one who's supposed to listen to the songs and practice them on the piano, it's my brother who jumps with delight whenever the music plays from the speakers. He's been accompanying me to my music lessons for over a year now, and all the songs are familiar to him. He sings along and moves his body, all smiley and happy, and his smile grows bigger when a song I've once practiced comes on.

"She can play this one!" he exclaims to my mother. "She can play this one!"

Among all the songs, "It's a Small World After All" is my brother's favourite. He even sings it on his own, and whenever the song is featured on a TV program, he runs to the screen and sings along to the end.

At music school, about ten children of my age take the weekly lessons together. There are rows of Electones in the classroom, and always, my two best friends and I sit next to each other on the left side of the room while other kids take seats on the right side of the room. Parents and younger siblings sit on the floors along the walls.

Once the class begins, my little brother plays with Karen's little sister. Being just a year younger than her, my brother likes following her wherever she goes.

During the class, I'm so busy listening to our teacher and chatting with my friends that I rarely pay attention to what my brother's up to. But once in while, the two toddlers become the focus of the whole class.

One day, my brother and Karen's sister go on a crawling adventure around the classroom. I don't think much about it until I feel something brush past my legs. Looking down, I find Karen's sister crawling under my chair, followed closely by another figure. My brother.

I refocus on my teacher, but this time, laughter ripples across the other side of the room. I turn to see two crawling figures travelling beneath my classmates' chairs. *What on earth are they doing?*

Our teacher is now explaining something about the music piece we're playing.

Suddenly, there's an explosion of laughter, and two crawling figures pass in front of our teacher. First, Karen's sister, then my brother. They must be having fun, giggling like crazy as they brush past our teacher's knees. The two of them seem to enjoy the spotlight of attention.

"That's enough!" Karen's mother dashes to the front and grabs her daughter. My mother follows suit.

Karen's sister and my brother are brought back to their original position by the wall and told to stay there. No more crawling happens after that. Yet I cannot help noticing the privilege enjoyed by our little siblings. Had I been a toddler about to crawl around the room, I'm sure my mother would've caught me before my hands and knees even hit the floor.

After the lesson, the nine of us cram into the five-seater to drive back home. The mother sitting on the front passenger seat is accompanied by two little ones: Karen's sister at her feet under the glove compartment, and my brother in her lap. We three girls are squeezed in the back seat along with one adult, on whose lap sits Sakura's baby brother.

The packed car carries us all back to our community of apartments – driving past the municipal court building and the Mercedes-Benz showcase, crossing the river, passing the art gallery and the post office, until the familiar apartment blocks come into our sight.

On the way, lollipops are distributed to everybody, and we girls chat about our play plan after reaching home as we lick the colourful candies. Adults are also busy talking, but about less interesting topics – tonight's supper plan and other things.

Our drive suddenly becomes thrilling when one of the mothers calls out, "Police are coming!"

Then we stop talking and quickly hide the four extra heads in the car so that they won't be visible from outside.

One day, my mother's seated in the back with us girls when somebody warns us there's a police car behind us.

"Duck your head, sweetie!" says my mother and covers my head with her arm, the excitement in her voice surprising me. "Police" sounds like a serious thing, but nobody seems worried. It's as if we're playing a game against them.

Once the danger passes, we spread our bodies again – as much as we can, that is – and enjoy the rest of our chaotic journey.

My Mother and Brother

These days, my brother is interested in helping our mother. Whenever I'm at kindergarten and she goes to buy our weekly milk at a corner store across the street, my brother accompanies her and insists on carrying the milk back home.

Our mother tries to talk him out of it, knowing the one-litre carton is too heavy for a two-year-old, but my brother won't listen. In the end, she gives up and hands him the plastic bag containing the milk carton.

Because the bag is indeed heavy, instead of lifting it, my brother drags it behind him. As he happily marches forward, one corner of the milk carton rubs against the asphalt through the thin plastic bag.

"*Thank you* for your help, sweetie!" our mother says delightedly once they're back home, gently taking the bag from my brother's hand. When he toddles off, beaming with a smile of pride, she quickly checks on the milk carton. Just as she thought, there's a tiny hole on the corner where it dragged on the ground. What a relief that they've arrived just in time to avoid any major leakage! She flips the milk carton upside down and puts it in the fridge.

My brother learns how to count numbers, and he wants to practice his new knowledge whenever and wherever possible. Every day, when he goes to the washroom with our mother to poop, while squatting over the toilet bowl, he holds out his hand and shapes it into a number.

"This is ... ONE!!"

Then he makes two with his fingers. "This is ... TWO!!"

My brother now makes three with his fingers. "This is ... THREE!!"

His counting continues until the moment he leaves the washroom.

Our next-door neighbour tells our mother that she often hears my brother's counting voice in the hallway between our apartments. She thinks it's lovely.

Our mother laughs. "I really don't understand why he has to count numbers in the washroom, of all the places in the world!"

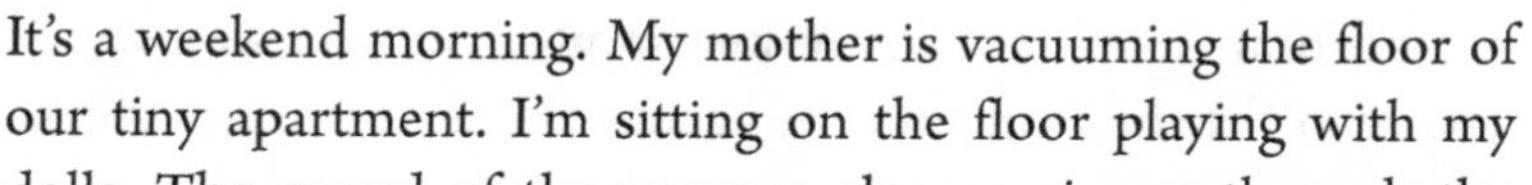

It's a weekend morning. My mother is vacuuming the floor of our tiny apartment. I'm sitting on the floor playing with my dolls. The sound of the vacuum cleaner pierces through the rooms, and I can hardly hear anything else. I try to concentrate on my dolls' conversation and the story unfolding among them.

Suddenly, my mother turns off the vacuum cleaner. The whole air stops vibrating and falls silent.

"Sweetie!" My mother's laugh echoes in the room. When I look up, I find my brother riding the main body of the cleaning device like he does his ride-on car. "You were the reason why I had a hard time pulling the vacuum cleaner!"

When did he come over? I don't know. But he's all smiley as he sits comfortably on top of the cleaner.

"Now, get off, please!" My mother ushers my brother off the vacuum cleaner, but he's laughing. From his face, I can tell he'll do it again.

Sure enough, as soon as my mother continues vacuuming with her back to the main device, my brother rides on it again. It's not until she tries to pull the device that my mother realizes my brother's sitting there. Ushering him off again, she tries distracting him this time.

"Why don't you play with your buses, sweetie?"

This has become our routine since my brother discovered the fun of riding the vacuum cleaner.

My brother now has his own study time with our mother. His task is to complete a few mazes in a toddler workbook.

The first time he tried it, our mother told me, he didn't understand the rule and connected the start point and the end point with a straight line. But these days, he knows what to do, and he can draw a path that avoids the dead ends in the maze.

Unlike me, my brother loves his study time. Every day, when our mother calls him for his study, he eagerly runs to the little table set up for him.

Other than the task itself, what my brother looks forward to is the applause he gets from our mother when he completes a maze.

"I'll do more! I'll do more!" he exclaims, standing up enthusiastically.

No sooner than she shows him a new maze, my brother dives in to work out the path.

A few mazes later, however, my brother's focus dwindles. Our mother notices and suggests they end the study session.

She wants to make sure my brother finishes with a sense of accomplishment. But he won't listen.

"I'll do more!" he insists. "I'll do more!"

So, she gives him another maze, knowing full well what will happen next.

A few minutes in, my brother hits a dead end. He cannot figure out how to continue, and his mood plummets.

"I *won't* do anymore!" he declares and disappears to the back room to play with his toy buses. Our mother, knowing better than to chase him, casually waits there, reading a newspaper.

Several minutes later, my brother comes back to the table, refreshed and ready to tackle the maze he couldn't finish. He succeeds this time. Our mother tells him to end the session for today, and this time, my brother agrees.

Every day, while I'm at kindergarten, my mother takes my brother out on a walk in the neighbourhood. He leads the walk on his yellow ride-on car and my mother walks closely behind him.

Their walk starts with a visit to the square playground in front of our apartment block, then continues toward the place that's most important to my brother. At the farthest end of our community, there's a hill, and on top of that hill is the small open area where out-of-service local buses come and stay until their next service hour. This is the place where my brother enjoys his bus-watching.

On a lucky day, they find a bus or two waiting in the parking lot. My brother then parks his ride-on car and observes the buses in detail – in particular, their colour descriptions – until they leave, or if that doesn't happen soon, my mother suggests it's time to go home.

On a less lucky day, there's no bus to be found in the parking lot. My brother then waits on his ride-on car with endless patience until finally a bus appears, or if that doesn't happen soon, my mother suggests that they go home.

On their way back down the hill, my brother likes to speed up on his ride-on car. Unlike me, he's fearless. He kicks the ground hard before letting gravity take him down the hill at high speed. Once this happens, my mother has no hope of catching up with him.

In the middle of the slope, there's a pothole. It's not huge, but large enough to catch the wheels of a ride-on car. One day after rain, as my brother drives down the slope at full speed, his ride-on car gets caught in the pothole and comes to a sudden halt, throwing him off hard to the ground, face down.

"I've told you, sweetie, haven't I?" gasps my mother when she finally catches up with my brother, who's now crying with his face muddy. "I told you not to go so fast! *This* is the reason. Now you've hurt yourself!"

Even after this painful incident, my brother continues to speed down the hill on his ride-on car. He now makes sure to avoid the pothole with his remarkable driving skill.

My brother is full of energy. Whenever he's not playing with his toy buses, he runs around our tiny apartment at high speed.

Although my mother has done her best to make our home hazard-free, due to the limited space, our living area is full of furniture edges. Not yet having good control over his body, my brother often bumps into one of those edges. Usually, it's his head or toe that gets caught and bruised.

The bruise is never really serious – in the worst case, maybe a tiny bump on his head.

"You'll be all right, sweetie," my mother consoles him when he comes to her crying. "The pain will soon pass."

But my brother isn't satisfied. He needs proper treatment for his bruise.

"I want a Band-Aid."

"A Band-Aid?" My mother repeats blankly. "But you're not bleeding, sweetie."

"I want a Band-Aid," insists my brother.

Seeing his determination, my mother takes out a Band-Aid and puts it on his cheek. "Do you feel better now?"

The effect of the Band-Aid is instant. My brother stops whining and goes back to playing as if nothing had happened.

A Band-Aid is my brother's miracle cure. It doesn't matter which part of his body is hurt or what kind of injury. A Band-Aid always makes him feel better. This is the reason why you often find a Band-Aid plastered somewhere on his face.

Kindergarten Sports Festival

Every afternoon, I eagerly wait for the end of my time at kindergarten. It's not that I don't like spending time with my classmates or my teachers. But I prefer being free and playing with my two best friends in our favourite tree or going on an adventure with my brother at home.

When the class is finally dismissed, I run outside. The playground is crowded with mothers and toddler siblings who've come to pick us up. After a quick scan, I spot my mother in her red jacket chatting with other mothers. My little brother is playing with Karen's little sister. With both of them occupied, there's some time to play before going home.

Thrusting my bag towards my mother, who absentmindedly takes it, I climb up the jungle gym with Sakura and Karen. That's where we stay until our mothers finally come out of their conversation and call our names. "Girls, time to go home!"

The kindergarten stands on a steep hill. As I skip down the road with my friends, I find our head teacher standing at the bottom of the slope with a yellow flag in her hand. She always does that to make sure all of us cross the road safely.

As we near the end of the slope, Karen's little sister breaks into a run. My brother follows her. Our head teacher turns around, her face bright with a smile and her arms wide open, ready to catch them in an embrace.

Karen's sister reaches her first and jumps into her arms. Then, it's my brother's turn. Just before reaching our head teacher, however, he stops. He stops in front of her open arms and cautiously studies her face without a smile. After a full moment of silent gaze, my brother carries on, without further interacting with her.

My friends and I greet our teacher in loud voices, and we all continue our walk back home.

Autumn arrives, and at my kindergarten, the annual sports festival takes place. There are several performances and races planned, but the one I'm most excited about is the dance I do with all my peers.

The theme of this year's sports festival is "dinosaurs." In our dance performance, we are wearing dinosaur costumes made of blue plastic bags, decorated with paper spikes on the back.

Our teachers have picked the music and come up with the choreography. In this dance, we form lines and move our bodies to the music while singing the song.

Not everybody is into this kind of activity. Some are shy, their movements reserved and their voices low. Others are okay with the idea of a dance performance. They move fine and sing fine. Then, there's me, who's totally into the world of dinosaurs our teachers have created, and becomes a dinosaur the moment we line up to dance. Once the music starts, I extend my arms and legs to the fullest, sing at my top voice, and when we roar in the middle of the performance, I'm ecstatic, feeling as if we're the coolest crowd of people on earth.

Later that day, my mother tells me how my performance stood out from everybody else.

"You were the only one who was actually being a dinosaur," she laughs. "Your movement was very convincing!"

The middle section of the sports festival is dedicated to various kinds of races. One of them is a race that we do with our fathers. We haven't practiced it, so I don't know what to expect.

"You're now going on an adventure to find dinosaur eggs," our head teacher explains to us before we go out on the track. "It's going to be a dangerous journey, I must warn you."

"Why?" several voices ask at the same time.

"Because there'll be dinosaurs. See, they're already waiting to eat you!" She points to the other side of the area, where large creatures, seemingly made of cardboard, roam around.

"The eggs you need to retrieve are on the other side of those dinosaurs. The good news is that there's a way to make them fall asleep."

"What is it?" somebody asks.

"Well, you make them eat a special pebble. Just before you meet the dinosaurs, pick one pebble from the pool, and put it in their mouth. Then you can pass safely."

I love this kind of mission. I'll be the first to come back with the dinosaur's egg!

"You'll have to collaborate with your father to successfully accomplish this mission," our teacher advises, and we all line up at the start point.

The pistol sounds, and my father and I begin the race alongside my friends and their fathers. We run, and in no time, come to the pebble pool. The pool is so close to the dinosaurs that teachers who stand nearby warn us to be very quiet. "You don't want to draw their attention!"

I pick up a pebble and see it is actually made of wadded-up paper. My father hoists me up on his shoulders so that I can throw the pebble into a dinosaur's mouth. There are several dinosaurs, but because there are many of us egg-hunters, we each only need to focus on one dinosaur.

When I sit on my father's shoulders, I become taller than the dinosaur in front of me, and I get the glimpse of the dinosaur's *inside*. What I find there is most unexpected: somebody's mother is operating the cardboard dinosaur! Gazing at the top of her head, I almost forget what I've been told to do.

"Have you thrown your pebble yet?" My father's voice grabs me out of stupor. "You're getting heavy here. Do it quickly!"

So I throw the paper pebble into the cardboard dinosaur operated by somebody's mother. I'm not sure if it made the dinosaur sleep, since she's still clearly moving. But a voice tells us from behind that the dinosaurs are now all asleep and that we must hurry.

We all run to the "bush," which is also made of cardboard and which hides a pool of dinosaur eggs.

"Pick one and run!" a teacher instructs us from somewhere nearby. "Before they awaken!"

The eggs are different sizes. I pick the largest one.

"Somebody's mother was in the dinosaur," I tell my father as we run toward the goal point, hand in hand. "Isn't that strange? Why is anybody in there?"

The race is over, and I'm left with a dinosaur egg. Its content turns out to be a soccer ball. I don't play soccer, but I love cuddling round objects, so I'm happy. The only thing I cannot understand is why I saw somebody's mother inside the dinosaur.

There's a race designed for our younger siblings, too. When they're called to the track with their parents, my brother stands at the start line with my mother and other toddlers. Many of them seem clueless what's going on, but once the pistol sounds, with their parents' nudges, they slowly cross the field to the other side. My brother also follows.

From where I sit, I cannot see their faces clearly, but I spot Karen's sister dashing to the goal line like a shooting star. My brother's toddling behind the crowd with my mother, looking unsure what this race is all about.

Once they reach the goal, our head teacher hands each of them a treat – a small snack item – and the race is over. My brother goes back to the family seating area with my mother, with his treat in his hand.

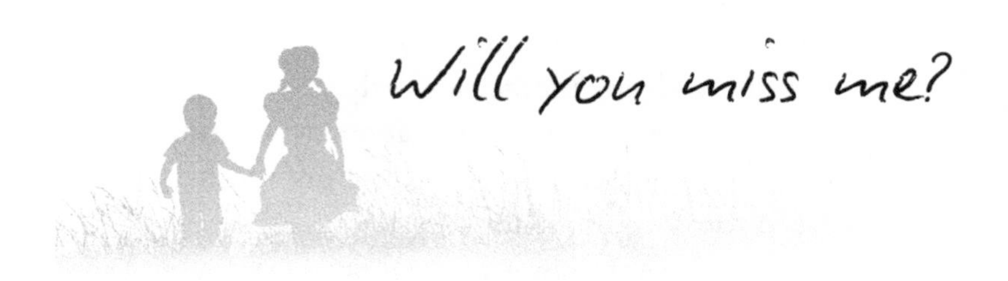

Will you miss me?

In our community of apartments, all six apartment blocks are numbered. Since ours is the oldest of all, its number is the youngest: number one.

On the side of our apartment block, the number one is printed in large black lettering. Whenever we go out, my brother sees it and says to everybody around him that our apartment block is number one. The number one starts carrying a special meaning to him.

One weekend morning, my brother and I are watching TV together. My favourite quiz program about insects is on. A female cartoon character appears on the screen dressed like an insect, and after a short video clip about an insect, she asks a question about its lifestyle followed by three answer choices.

Standing in front of the screen, I think about the question and give my answer aloud. "I go for number two!"

Next to me, my brother quickly shouts his answer, too. "I go for number one!"

It doesn't matter what the question is. My brother always chooses number one.

A few times, after giving my first answer, I have a second thought. "I change my mind! I go for number three!"

"I change my mind!" my brother exclaims with a beaming smile. "I go for number ONE!"

Such is his obsession with number one.

At kindergarten, my friends and I are currently into something called spool knitting. Teacher Mina has taught us how to do it using part of an empty milk carton and disposable chopsticks. She gave us each a ball of yarn, showed us how to spin the first layer along the chopsticks, then left us to continue at our own pace.

My yarn is brown. Every day, I sit with my friends and carefully pass my yarn around the five chopstick poles attached to the milk carton. After a while, my hands learn the motion, and I can do it without thinking. I chat with my friends while knitting, and that's one of the most satisfying things I can think of right now. At the end of each day, I look at the brown woolen cylinder getting longer under my milk package and celebrate the day's progress.

I can make this into a muffler, teacher Mina says. Once it's long enough, she'll teach me how to close the ends and help me attach woolen pom-poms. I cannot wait for that day to come. As my brown woolen cylinder gets longer, my knitting pace also picks up. I even knit at home in the evening.

Then, one day, teacher Mina sees my knitting and says it's ready to be made into a muffler. In front of my eager eyes, she closes the two ends of my brown woolen cylinder and attaches a blue pom-pom at each end.

"There we go," she says, handing me my completed muffler. "You did a great job! Now you can wear your beautiful muffler!"

When it's time for me to go home, I run outside to find my mother and brother with my brand-new hand-knit muffler around my neck. "Look!" I can barely control my excitement. "My muffler! I made it! It even has pom-poms!"

My mother says I've done a great job and that the muffler looks good on me. I'm so happy that I jump around.

Once we get back home, however, I realize I don't like wearing a muffler in general. I toss my brown muffler into my toy box among many plush dolls. It's my brother who finds interest in my creation. He wears the muffler at home, and it becomes an essential item for him whenever he pretends to go out shopping, mimicking our mother.

My mother does her daily grocery shopping at shops across the street. Sometimes my brother and I accompany her, but more often, we stay at home.

Before leaving, my mother always says the same thing. "Sweeties, I'm now going out for shopping. But don't worry, I'll be back *very soon*!"

My mother often forgets some things at home. On those occasions when we accompany her, we hear her exclaim, "Oh, shoot! I forgot!"

But she rarely heads back home to fetch the item since she also tends not to worry about small matters. Instead, we hear her say, "Oh, well, never mind!" She then carries on with her shopping, without whatever she's left at home.

My brother's lately into mimicking others around him, and my mother's shopping routine has caught his attention.

Every now and then, my brother puts my brown muffler around his neck and declares he's now going out shopping. When my mother gives him a yellow wallet and a plastic bag, my brother carefully places the wallet on the floor.

Once ready, with the empty plastic bag in his hand, my brother turns to us. "I'm now going out shopping. Oh, but don't worry, I'll be back *very soon*!"

No sooner than he's closed the imaginary door, he stops and exclaims. "Oh, shoot! I forgot my wallet!"

As my mother and I watch him in anticipation, my brother beams with a smile. "Oh, well! Never mind!" He then carries on with his shopping without his wallet.

It's funny that among all things, my brother chooses the wallet as the item to leave behind because it's the one thing that my mother does mind whenever she forgets it.

In any case, my brother's shopping performance is greatly enjoyed by the audience. My mother's an especially big fan of the show, always rolling with laughter.

Since I entered kindergarten, I catch a cold more frequently than before. Whenever I become sick, my mother prepares a futon for me in the back room and tells my brother to stay in the other room so that he doesn't contract the virus.

When my mother goes out for an errand, I can hear my brother play with his toy buses in the next room. After a while, however, his voice stops and the room becomes silent. As I wonder what he's up to, I hear footsteps, and my brother appears at the door.

"If I'm gone, will you miss me?" He's obeying our mother, so only his head is visible.

"Yes, of course I'll miss you," I reply.

Satisfied, my brother goes back to play with his buses. Then after some time, his voice stops again, and I hear his footsteps. He pokes his head through the doorway and asks me again, "If I'm gone, will you miss me?"

"Of course I'll miss you."

My brother's face wrinkles with a smile. "Then I'll *always* be here."

This ritual continues until my brother forgets my mother's words and starts visiting my bedside to play with me.

Some time after both my brother and I become sick, my mother takes us to the city hospital. She registers us at the reception desk, and we wait in the hallway on one of the countless brown benches.

For some reason, by the time we get to the hospital, I'm not feeling too sick anymore. While we wait for our turn, my brother and I roam around the hallway, exploring different benches and watching people sitting on them.

When my mother calls us, we all go into the paediatrician's room at the far end of the corridor. My mother speaks with the doctor, and the doctor examines us. She scribbles things on her clipboard, and we leave the room.

Then comes the long waiting period once again. But this time, an exciting plan awaits us.

Next to the reception desk is a staircase that leads to the basement where a row of vending machines stands. "Sweetie, get a juice from the vending machine downstairs," says my mother, handing me a few coins from her purse. "It's a treat for you."

Holding the coins tight, I run down to the basement. There's a variety of juices in the vending machine, but I already know which one I want: apple juice.

I insert the coins my mother gave me, and press the button for a package of apple juice. As soon as the package drops in the dispenser with a thud, I grab it and run back upstairs.

While I was getting my juice, my mother has given my brother a toddler apple juice she brought from home. Each holding a package of apple juice, my brother and I walk over to the windows at the end of the hallway.

We both stand there, sipping the juice and gazing out of the window at the parking outside. This is my favourite moment of the hospital visit. We forget about everything else and get lost in the apple juice magic until my mother calls us again. It's now time to go home.

My brother takes a nap every afternoon. When it's time for his nap, my mother plays Pachelbel's "Canon" on our CD player, a daily cue that informs everyone at home what's about to happen next.

Every day, as soon as the first note of Pachelbel's "Canon" plays from the speaker, my brother becomes rebellious. "I'm not sleeping!" He raises his chin and protests. "I'm NOT sleeping!"

He goes to play with his toy buses, demonstrating that he's not sleepy. But my mother has a plan in place for this scenario. "Okay, then, your sister and I are going to sleep now. Let's go!"

My mother motions me to the back room where she's prepared a futon for my brother's nap. We then both lie down on the mattress for a few minutes before my brother feels lonely in the living room and comes to join us. His attitude is still rebellious, though. He won't just lie down.

"I'll sleep in Mommy's lap." He climbs onto my mother's lap and closes his eyes. But since it's not a comfortable position, he cannot fall asleep. He spends a while tossing and turning before finally giving up and settling on the mattress instead.

Several minutes later, I feel a tap on my shoulder.

"Wake up!" my mother whispers. "We'll start your study!"

As I get out of my blanket, I look at my sleeping brother and wonder why he hates his nap time so much. It's a privilege I'd gladly switch places for.

The Autumn

Today, my family are going to visit my paternal grandmother's house. She lives near Tokyo, and I'm excited to travel there by bullet train.

Since we're going to the national capital region, my mother dresses me and my brother in good clothes. I wear a dress instead of a sweater and a pair of trousers, and my brother his signature blue jeans with a green sweater.

Our trip is scheduled in the afternoon after my father comes home from work. That morning, my mother decides to take pictures of us for the New Year cards because it's rare for us to be dressed so properly.

The three of us walk past the square playground, heading toward my brother's favourite bus-watching spot on the hilltop. On the way, we stop under some cypress trees to pose for a few pictures.

"Sweetie," says my mother to my brother. "Imagine a bus goes by. What do you say?"

After several failed attempts, my brother finally responds with an excited face. "Oh! There goes a bus!"

I grin next to him, and my mother releases the shutter.

As the three of us continue our walk toward the hilltop, however, I realize something is off. All of a sudden, my body is out of energy and I don't want to move, like when I catch a cold.

I won't admit that, though. We're about to go on an exciting trip on the bullet train. How can I fall sick now? I try to look fine, faking my energetic self. But there's one person I cannot fool: my mother.

"Are you feeling unwell, sweetie?" She puts aside her camera, her eyes sharp with concern.

"I'm fine!" I reply quickly, putting on a cheerful face when really, all I want is to lie down anywhere right at this moment.

My mother doesn't believe my words. The photo session is dismissed, and we all head back home. Upon our return, my mother immediately puts a thermometer under my armpit. Sure enough, I have a fever. A high fever. I'm quickly carried to bed, and our trip is cancelled.

I'm crushed under disappointment as I stare at the ceiling of the back room. *Why today?* I ask myself over and over. It was such a special trip that I wanted to go even if I had to fake health.

Autumn deepens, and it's that time of the year again when we start thinking about Santa Claus and what we want for the Christmas. This year, I know exactly what I want. I want a toy from the Sailor Moon anime series. Specifically, the one called Stallion Rêve, the elegant round object with a green leg used by Chibi Moon to communicate with the flying horse. Ever since I saw its toy version in a TV ad, I cannot stop thinking about it.

Every night, I eagerly whisper, "Please, Santa Claus, bring me the Stallion Rêve this Christmas." Because I doubt Santa Claus watches the Sailor Moon series, I make sure to give him a detailed description of the item. "It's that round object used to communicate with the winged horse," I explain. "You know, the one with the green leg."

This year, my brother also has a request for Santa Claus. He wants a toy train, like the one he's seen at Sakura's house. It belongs to her little brother, but whenever we visit their apartment, my brother holds the toy train and doesn't leave it until we go home. He's as obsessed with the toy train as he is with his toy buses.

"Santa Claus," my brother's loud voice echoes in our tiny apartment. "I want a toy train. I'll be a good boy. Please bring me a toy train!"

I'm usually discreet about my wish, but when I hear my brother's loud wish, I make sure to express mine in a louder voice, too, so that Santa Claus won't forget about my request.

Although my brother and I get along well most of the times, there are moments when our disagreement over a small matter turns into a fight.

Our fight often happens in the same spot: in front of the digital piano in our living room. We're sitting on the floor facing each other when my brother grabs the toy I'm playing with and refuses to return it.

"Give it back!" I say, reaching for my toy.

But my brother doesn't listen. Instead, he smacks my face.

My brother is only two years old, and his slap isn't that powerful. It barely hurts. *This is nothing,* I tell myself in my head. *This is really nothing, I won't cry.* But there's something terribly sad about being hit by my younger brother. Despite my determination, tears roll down my cheeks, and I break into a loud cry.

My mother sees us from the kitchen and intervenes. "Sweetie, apologize to your sister."

My brother's clearly not happy with the idea. Apologizing to me in front of our mother is probably the last thing he wants to do. He remains silent, turning his eyes here and there, trying not to look at me. But my mother doesn't let it pass. "Did you say sorry?"

After a long pause, my brother blurts out, "Sorry." His tone is curt and his eyes are trained on the floor between us.

My mother now switches to a kinder voice. "Apologize properly, dear."

That's when my brother bursts into tears, his face turned upward, red and wrinkled. "I'm sorry."

My mother then comes around to give him a big hug.

Kindergarten Rummage Sale

One autumn weekend, an annual rummage sale takes place at my kindergarten. My mother leaves for the kindergarten early that morning to help out. She'll be overseeing one of the stalls.

A few hours later, my father, my brother and I walk to the kindergarten together. This is the second rummage sale I've participated in. At my first rummage sale, I got a beautiful red heart plush. I wonder what new plush doll I'll find at this one.

Today, my kindergarten looks different. With decorations everywhere and merry music playing, the place is like a fairground. Both the front garden and the classrooms are bustling with people of all ages. Quickly changing shoes at the shoe rack, we go inside.

In the back corridor behind the classrooms, just in front of the staircase, I find a small pool full of water balloons. A group of boys are huddled over, talking to someone who's in charge of the stall. Just as I join the crowd and peek at the pool from above, trying to see the colours of the balloons, I spot a familiar figure crouched by the pool. My mother! She's the one showing different balloons to the boys.

I've never seen my mother selling things before. She looks cool manning the water balloon stall! Taking out my wallet, I purchase two balloons from her, one for myself and one for my brother.

While I was busy with the water balloons, my father and brother have gone somewhere else. After searching the corridor, I figure they might've gone to the front garden. I walk through one of the classrooms – my classroom, actually – to get to the outside, when a stall of stuffed animals snags my attention.

"Do you want to have a look?" two mothers in charge of the stall call out to me.

I walk over, and my heart is immediately captured by a large plush dog. It has such a fluffy tail, and the size makes it look like a real dog. The two mothers help me pay, and I walk away with a new plush dog in my arms.

As soon as I come out into the front garden, I spot my father and brother walking my way. My father carries a package of fried noodles and a bag of popcorn.

"OK, sweeties," my father calls. "That was fun. Now, let's get going, shall we?"

It's been a brief visit, but we all got what we wanted. The three of us leave the rummage sale and walk home. On the way, we sit on the concrete wall surrounding our community to eat the noodles my father bought for us. As we eat, I show my father my new toy.

"This dog is cute!" I cannot stop smiling. "I'm so happy I got this."

Taking a close look at the plush doll, however, my father tells me something surprising. "I think this is a fox, sweetie, not a dog."

"A fox?" I repeat blankly. I've never seen a fox in my life except in picture books. My father explains that a fox has a long, fluffy tail and a pointed nose. Just like the plush doll I'm holding in my hands.

"I got a fox." I repeat to myself the name of the animal. Even if it's not a dog, I'm still in love with my new plush animal.

When we finish eating, my brother says he wants to watch buses, so the three of us head over to the hilltop on the far end of our community. Having no interest in buses, I perch on a metal pipe and watch my father and brother entertain themselves with the comings and goings of the buses. While I'm eating fresh popcorn with my new fox plush in my arms, a smile of satisfaction spreads on my face.

At my kindergarten, our teachers often take us to a walk in the neighbourhood. Since most of us live in the neighbourhood, we almost always encounter some of our family members. Our teacher then calls out to us, "Oh, there's so-and-so's father! Let's say hello, everyone!" or "Oh, that's so-and-so's mother and little sister! Say hello!"

I always look forward to these moments because it's exciting to learn about my classmates' families. But whoever happens to run into their own family members always turns their face away, looking embarrassed. And I wonder what there is to feel shy about.

One day during the walk, our head teacher tells us that my father is walking ahead of us. I spot my father crossing the street with his workbag, looking embarrassed to receive the attention of a group of kindergarteners, but managing a smile on his face. I'm so far back in the line that I don't think he sees me.

Another day, we're taking a walk in my community when we come across my mother and brother near the row of Japanese plum trees. They're probably on their way to the hilltop for bus-watching. My brother is sitting on his yellow ride-on car and my mother is smiling behind him in her red jacket.

My brother watches us curiously as if a festival has come his way. My mother waves at our group. I'm not sure if they see me or not.

"Maiko has a brother!" somebody shouts.

Yes, of course I do! I'm surprised by such an obvious statement. *That's my brother!*

But I don't say anything. Instead, I turn away just like others did upon encountering their family members.

The Yellow Dictionary

One evening after supper, my father says we're going to a bookstore to buy a Japanese dictionary for me. My family rarely goes out for shopping that late, so I get excited.

"What is a dictionary?" I ask.

"It's something useful when you read a book. You'll see!"

The four of us – my mother, father, brother and I – hop into the car and head over to the city centre, to one of the shopping arcades. Once we park the car, I follow my parents into the familiar bookstore. There aren't many large bookstores in town, and we always come to this one whenever we buy new books.

Tonight, however, my father leads us not to the usual children's books section, but to a shelf where many thick books are stocked. In front of my curious eyes, he grabs a few thick books, flipping through the pages as if comparing them, then decides on the one with a yellow cover.

"This should be good!" says my father cheerfully and ushers us all to the checkout.

I couldn't have told any difference between the contents of those thick books, but I like the fact that the one my father picked has a bright cover and it's thicker than others. Thick books are great, especially the satisfaction I get when flipping through the pages.

As soon as we're back in the car, my father takes out the brand-new book from the paper bag. "So, sweetie, this is what we call a Japanese dictionary. In this book, you can look up the meaning of a word you don't know. This dictionary is designed for children, so you'll be able to use it, too. Let's see..."

My father opens a page and places the book between us. With the help of the streetlight, we can read what's written.

"For example, I've just looked up the word *yamamorigohan* – 'a bowlful of rice.' Let's see what's written here."

He reads the description aloud and points to the illustration next to it. It's a picture of a bowl full of rice. In fact, the bowl is so full that the rice towers over it like a little mountain. I gaze at the illustration intently. But before I can read any further, my father quickly closes the book. "It's not good for your eyes to read in the car. Wait until we get back home."

Unfortunately, I never use the dictionary for the correct purpose since I'm too lazy to look up words while reading, even when I come across a new word. I prefer to imagine the meaning myself. Instead, I use my dictionary when I want to hold a thick book in my hands and flip through the pages to enjoy the feeling and the fragrance of the paper.

My Father and Brother

When it comes to wearing socks, there are two kinds of people on this planet: those who carefully arrange each sock so that the toe goes to the toe and the heel goes to the heel, and those who don't give any thought to it. My father belongs to the second group. He never minds the orientation of his socks as long as they cover his feet.

But my little brother isn't like that.

When my father puts the toddler socks on my brother's feet, oftentimes, the heels of the socks are facing upward. My brother never ignores it.

"Weird! Weird!" he calls out, pointing to his socks, until somebody comes around and fixes them for him.

My brother is a mommy's boy. Because he spent a long time with my mother at the hospital for his heart surgeries, he's very attached to her and doesn't like to be left without her. This can become a problem when my father has to look after my brother alone.

Two mornings a week, my father and brother stay at home alone while my mother goes to work and I go to kindergarten.

This father-son time isn't without its perks, but the air grows ominous when my brother starts asking for my mother with more and more urgency.

Finally, my father's patience runs out. He snaps, "Mommy won't come back!"

This is the last word they exchange.

Sometime later, my mother comes home. The moment the lock turns on the front door, signaling her return, my brother runs to the hallway, his lips pursed. My mother only needs to look at his expression and the messy room to know what's happened between him and my father. One simple question will confirm it.

"What's the matter, sweetie?"

That's when my brother bursts into tears, burying himself in our mother's arms.

A chocolate cornet is a Japanese pastry with a chocolate cream filling. The pastry is a shared favourite of my father's and brother's.

A travelling bakery visits our neighbourhood every Thursday morning, when my mother is at work and I'm at kindergarten. Whenever the truck arrives with its merry music, my brother is the first to notice. "Daddy, listen!" He jumps up and down in the room, his face lit up. "They're here!"

The two of them walk down the street to buy one chocolate cornet from the bakery. Once back home, my father divides the pastry into two halves. The pastry is cone-shaped, and one end is wider than the other. Though my brother is still a toddler, he's already aware enough to want to take the wider side. So, after dividing the pastry, my father takes the narrow part and gives the wider part to my brother – but always with one trick. He scoops up the chocolate filling from the wider portion and adds it to his side before handing the other to my brother.

My father likes reading books whenever he's at home. He starts reading his book sitting on the family couch. But since the couch is hard and far from comfortable, his body slowly slides down, and in no time, he's lying on the floor with his book held above his face.

This is typically when my brother comes along and gets inspired. He picks up my yellow Japanese dictionary and lies down next to our father. He then opens a random page and holds the dictionary over his face, mimicking our father.

"Look who's reading books!" My mother passes by and exclaims. "Two people are engaged in their reading!"

My brother giggles, and my father's concentration is also broken. I'm watching them from nearby, and burst into laugher, too.

Thanksgiving

Sometime in November, my brother is admitted to the large hospital for a close examination of his heart condition. Another major heart surgery will be taking place next spring, and this exam is part of the preparation.

As always, my mother accompanies my brother, taking many of his favourite toys and books, and tries her best to make his days at hospital feel as normal as possible.

During the day, my brother plays with his toy buses and his Pooh bear plush, or reads the *Nontan* series and his other favourite books. In the late afternoon, before supper, he watches TV – "With Mommy," "Play in English!" and the ninja boys anime series – all the programs we usually watch together at home. In the evening, he takes a bath alone while my mother helps him on the side. Once in the bathtub, he dances in a circle with toys in his hands.

"Anything, everything, tick, tick, tick!"

No matter how much daily routine my mother maintains around him, however, my brother knows he's staying at the hospital, and everything is different from when he's at home.

"It's not you and me here," he explains to my mother one day as he plays with his Pooh bear plush on his bed. "We're at home. It's Daddy and Big Sister staying at the hospital."

While my mother and brother are away, my father and I stay at home by ourselves for several days. By now, we're both familiar with the routine when it's just the two of us. Simple toasted bread for breakfast, a day at kindergarten, then playtime with my friends, and in the evening, my father and I go out to one of the tiny diners in the neighbourhood to eat dinner.

Without my brother, at home, I play with my dolls, read books, watch my regular TV programs – "With Mommy," "Play in English!" and the ninja boys anime series – and once I've done all these things, I look for something else to busy myself with. This is often when I pick up my art and craft bag and work on a creative project.

When my brother was born, I used to have plastic toy fruits. What if I make them with origami paper this time? They'll make a perfect gift for my mother and brother when we visit them at the hospital.

I sit in the corner of the back room with a bagful of origami paper, a pair of scissors and a tube of glue and set out to create the shapes of different fruits. An apple, grapes, a banana, an orange… As I fold the colourful paper, my heart leaps with excitement. I cannot wait to complete all the paper fruits and bring them to my mother and brother. What will they say when they see my creations? Soon, I'm so absorbed in my project that everything else disappears from my world.

I have no idea how much time has passed when I finally finish. I'm happy with the way they've turned out. I grab the red plastic basket from my toy box – the one that used to carry my toy fruits – and collect all my paper fruits in it.

The next day, my father and I visit the hospital to see my mother and brother. The moment the elevator door opens, I find them sitting on the bench in the hallway, waiting for us. My brother is the first to spot us and run forward.

I normally play with him right away, but today, there's something important to show him: my paper fruits. I carefully take them out from the red basket. "Look what I've made for you!"

My brother is probably too small to appreciate my artwork. Though he likes real fruit, he shows little interest in paper ones. But my mother is intrigued.

"Wow!" she exclaims. There's a hint of surprise to her voice as she takes my creations in her hands. She's always impressed by my art and craft activities, but today, her surprise sounds more than usual. She takes a closer look. "You made these from origami paper?"

"Yes!"

"How amazing," says my mother with awe. "They look like real fruit!"

Hearing my mother's compliment, my face shines with pride.

"Why don't you bring them to kindergarten, sweetie?" my mother continues. "They're so beautiful. Your teacher would love to see them, too."

I haven't thought of that. But if my mother says so, why not?

The next day, I bring my paper fruits to kindergarten. Teacher Mina asks me if she can keep them for some time. Though not sure what she plans to do with them, I agree because the request feels like an honour.

A few days later, the Thanksgiving service is held at my Protestant kindergarten. When I go upstairs to the prayer room for the gathering, I find a large basket of fruit displayed on the main table. The table carries a special decoration to celebrate Thanksgiving, and it looks familiar...

My eyes widen with disbelief. They're my paper fruits! Somebody used them to decorate the side of the main table!

During the service, I cannot take my eyes off the table. I think back on my visit to the hospital yesterday and the conversation I had with my mother. Nobody in this room knows about it, the little secret hidden behind the colourful decorations on the table.

The Winter

One day in early December, my mother takes out a box containing our Christmas tree from the storage and brings it to the living room of our apartment. It's a small fake Christmas tree my parents bought when we moved into the apartment four years ago.

The plastic tree comes in several parts. As my mother assembles the trunk and the branches, slowly, the shape of a fir tree appears, and that's when my brother and I come running to the room, abandoning whatever we've been doing.

"Mommy, are you doing the Christmas tree?"

The Christmas tree kit comes with tiny ornaments, some tinsel, fluffy cotton to mimic snow, and a large star to be placed on top. After my mother finishes assembling the tree, the three of us spend some time decorating it together, hanging the ornaments on different branches, sticking the cotton between the branches, and wrapping the tree with the shiny tinsel. Since my brother isn't tall enough to reach far up, I'm the one who places the star on the treetop.

From that day on, the Christmas tree becomes the centre of my brother's and my attention. I pretend to be a horse, eating the tree leaves. I then become a cat with my brother, cozying up under the tree. Various ornaments hanging from the tree come in handy – I pick some apple-shaped ornaments for our food and a candle for warmth. We also pretend to be a prince and a princess by wearing the tinsel and cotton on our clothes.

On Christmas morning, my brother and I wake up early. In the living room, I can hear the sound of the stove, but other than that, it's all quiet.

We both jump out of the blankets and walk through the open sliding door between the two rooms. My mother is sitting there. But today, neither of us pays attention to her. Our eyes go straight to the Christmas tree in the corner. Underneath the tree is ... a pile of presents covered in shiny wrapping paper.

"Santa Claus!" we both shout as we rush the tree. "He came!"

"He did," says my mother, watching us with a smile. "That's because you've been good children! He left presents for you."

She tells us which one is for whom – Santa must have left a message for her – and my brother and I each take a package and rip the paper wrapping.

"My Stallion Rêve!" I cry, holding the box with the Sailor Moon toy I've wanted for so long.

"My train!" cries my brother, holding the large metal toy train in his hands.

The rest of the morning is a blur. We're so happy with our dream toys that we keep playing with them and talking about them. Even during the family dinner, we don't let them go.

One day, shortly after Christmas, I wake up to find everything outside covered in white snow. It's not the first snowfall, but it's the first time the snow has stayed on the ground this winter. From the balcony, I can see the white snow reflecting the bright sunlight everywhere – on the trees, on the ground, on the cars, and on the apartment blocks where my friends live.

After breakfast, my mother takes me and my brother to the square playground to enjoy the snow.

Today, I'm wearing a pale blue jacket with a fluffy hood, not my usual purple one. Its colour is a perfect match to the silvery world around us.

Once on the playground, my brother and I run in the snow. Nobody has walked on the ground yet, and there's not even a single footprint before us.

"Hurray!" we scream as we run. "We're the first!"

My mother has brought her film camera to take our photos in the snow. As we run around in the park, she calls us to pose. I raise my hand, stretching two fingers in front of my forehead like Sailor Moon and place the other on my waist.

After some time, my mother calls us to go home.

"So soon?" my brother and I protest as we run back to join my mother at the playground entrance. The three of us head back home, and I think about our next activity of the day.

In the New Year, my mother, brother, and I visit my grandmother's house. One day, my brother and I are sitting on the soft couch in the sun room when my grandmother appears with a beautiful red kimono in her hands.

"This used to belong to your mother when she was your age," she explains to me as she spreads out the kimono in front of us. "Would you like to try it on?"

Whatever has occupied my mind disappears in that moment. Wearing this kimono? Like a real princess?

"I want to wear it!" I jump to my feet, my eyes wide with excitement.

"Then come this way. I'll help you."

I follow my grandmother into the adjacent room, where she skillfully wraps the kimono around my body, adjusts the length, then pulls together the two sides of the front and secures them with a cord. Finally, she covers it with a beautiful belt.

"There you go." She smiles up at me. "See how pretty you look!"

I shuffle to the mirror. As soon as I find my reflection, my face shines with delight. "I look like a princess!" I exclaim. "Look, I'm a princess!"

"You're a proper princess," comes back my grandmother's voice. "Wait here. I'll also wear a kimono so that I can look good sitting with you."

With that, she disappears into her room. My brother toddles around me, but I'm busy checking out my princess look in the mirror and making different poses.

When my grandmother returns dressed in a kimono – a dark-coloured one – she no longer looks like my grandmother. She looks like a princess, too!

"Oh, don't you two look fabulous!" My mother comes in with her camera. "Sit there together so that I can take a picture of you both!"

My grandmother and I sit on the floor with our hands folded on our laps. When my mother tells us to smile, I respond with a tight-lipped smile. Being a real princess, I dare not open my mouth. My grandmother finds my princess gesture funny, and she's on the verge of laughing as my mother releases the shutter.

On the way back home, we take a local train to the Oyama station where we catch the bullet train back to Sendai. Normally, we wait on the platform, but today, our train is delayed. My mother takes us to the waiting room located one level below the platform.

The station is never really busy, but this waiting room is even quieter. Today, we're the only occupants. The room is plain, and no source of entertainment is provided. Only the benches.

As soon as we settle in the middle of the room, my mother opens her backpack to take out our regular snacks – toddler biscuits, candies, and our favourite Muscat grape chewing gum. At first, my brother and I remain on the bench like well-behaved children. But it doesn't take long before our abundant energy steals the calm away. We leave our spots and run around the empty waiting room with the packages of chewing gum in our hands.

Once in a while, we circle back to our mother to ask the same question. "Is our train coming yet?"

Her answer is the same. "No, not yet."

By the time she finally stands up and waves at us, my brother and I have thoroughly explored the waiting room so that even each single dust speck would've been familiar to us.

"Sweeties, let's go!"

As soon as my mother calls us, we dash back to join her. It's finally time to leave this too-plain room and ready ourselves for an exciting train ride.

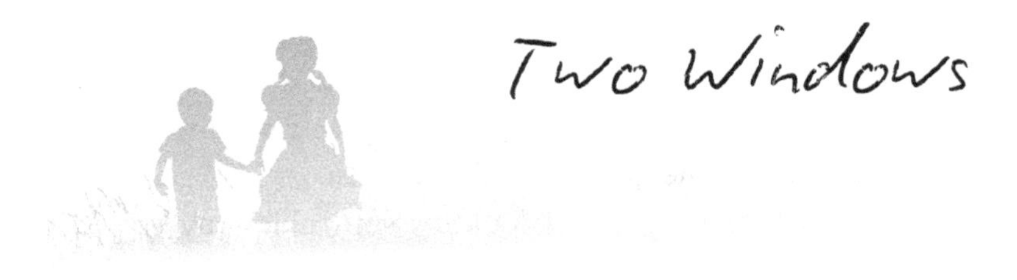

Two Windows

One fine winter day, my mother gives us a permission to blow bubbles on the balcony of our apartment. Excited by this rare opportunity, my brother and I run to the balcony. We each hold a bright pink bottle of bubble solution and a wand in our hands.

"Bubbles, bubbles..."

I dip my wand in the liquid. Just one blow, and many tiny bubbles come out of my wand, which makes me want to scream in excitement. Next to me, my brother also blows into his wand, releasing many small bubbles into the cold winter air.

"Hurray! Today is our bubbles day!"

In no time, the entire balcony is filled with the bubbles we've produced, and some wander off inside the house through the open door. It's extraordinary to see the round, shiny bubbles float around in our familiar living room. As if somebody had called in magic.

A brilliant idea occurs to me.

Fighting a giggle, I face my wand toward the open balcony doorway and blow through it. The tiny bubbles are quick to conquer the living room. My brother follows suit. Together, we blow bubbles inside the house.

"Stop, stop, stop, STOP IT!" My mother shuffles out of the kitchen. "You must face *that* way! Don't blow your bubbles into the room!"

We pretend we understood her, but as soon as she goes back inside, we again face toward the living room and blow bubbles in there. It's fun to watch bubbles dance around our living room and to see our mother getting upset by them.

After a while, I get bored and by controlling my breath, I start blowing huge bubbles instead of tiny ones. My brother's still having fun sending tiny bubbles into the living room. My mother has given up on disciplining us. Instead, she now takes pictures of us blowing bubbles on the balcony.

Through the open window of the back room of our apartment, the cool morning air sweeps in. I'm running around the room with my little brother when suddenly, I get inspired to go to the next room – the tiniest room, used for storage. Being afraid of the dark, I never go in there at night, but now, in the bright daylight, the room is just like any other.

I dash into the storage room followed by my brother. Together, we go to the far end of the room where the window is open. I poke out my head to see what view I can get from this window. It's mostly the same as the one I see from the back room, but slightly shifted to the left. When I turn my head to the right, I see the open window of the back room.

Suddenly, a fun idea occurs to me.

"You wait here," I tell my brother. "I'll go to the other room and wave at you from that window."

My brother seems to like this idea. He happily stays behind as I run to the next room.

Once I get to the window, I poke out my head and look to the left. "Are you there?"

Immediately, my brother's smiley face pops out from the other window. "Hello!"

"Hello!"

We wave at each other. Even though we're just a few feet apart, there's an awareness that we're in different rooms, which excites me. It feels like a secret communication!

My brother and I switch places and continue greeting until finally we're both satisfied and ready to move on to our next activity.

One morning, I find my mother on the balcony, hanging blankets on the railing. She does this whenever it's sunny outside, but today is the first time I'm intrigued by it.

As I gaze through the open glass doors at the thick blankets swaying in the wind, I suddenly wonder: *What if I go behind that blanket? Would it feel like a hidden nest?*

No sooner than the thought occurs to me, I dash toward the balcony barefoot. My brother follows me.

The moment I slip behind the hanging blanket, solid darkness envelops me. "Wow, it's night here!" I exclaim. "It's amazing!"

The blanket ripples, and my brother appears next to me. "Wow, it's night here!"

We both sit down and take in the darkness around us. How fun is it that we can experience night when it's still daytime outside. Plus, this place is hidden. It's a secret world for the two of us.

"Who's hiding there?" comes my mother's voice. "I can see two pairs of feet!"

"That's not us, Mommy!" I call out. "Because we cannot see you! It's night here!"

"It's night here!" echoes my brother next to me.

"And it's amazing!"

"It's amazing!"

We then burst into laughter, elated by our new discovery. Little do we know that our mother is taking a picture of our feet sticking out below the hanging blanket.

The skating season has arrived. When my family does our regular weekend shopping at the mall, my father takes me to the indoor skating rink again. Though I'm excited, because it's been a long time since I stood on the rink last time and learned how to skate, I struggle to even stand on the ice at first.

While my father skates around the rink, I carefully review the basics. Holding the railing, I remember how to balance myself on the ice and how to move. Slowly, my body recalls the feeling of gliding on the ice as well as the fun of it.

Then, one day, something new happens. My mother and brother come along to join us on the rink for the first time. My mother says my brother is now old enough to try out skating.

Covered in a thick jacket, my brother sits on the bench looking puzzled. He has no idea what's going on or what fun awaits him. When my mother tries to put the skates on his feet, he doesn't like it. He relaxes his feet, making it hard for my mother to slide his feet into the shoes.

I don't know how, but after awhile, my mother succeeds at putting the skates on my brother's reluctant feet. As I make a loop around the rink, I spot my father pushing my brother on a metal supporter near the entrance. What they're doing doesn't look like skating, but they seem to be having fun. When I finish a loop and do another one, I encounter them again moving on the ice, making a lot of noise.

Some time passes, and my mother calls out that it's time for us to go home. After making a final loop around the rink, I come back to the seating area to remove my skates.

My brother and father also come back to the bench. That's when my brother discovers something extraordinary – he can stand on the floor in his skates, without anybody supporting him!

"Look!" he calls out to everyone, his eyes wide with delight. "Look!"

"Wow!" my mother responds to his exclamation. "How amazing, sweetie! You're standing on your own!" She then tells him to sit down so that she can remove his skates. But my brother isn't listening. Now that he's so into his skates, he doesn't want to remove them.

"Look!" he repeats, standing straight and proud. "Look!"

It takes my brother a lot of convincing before he finally sits down and my mother can take the skates off his feet. But even after getting back to his normal shoes, my brother's excitement lives on. On the way back home, he keeps reminding us how he stood on the floor in his skates.

One afternoon, I come home from kindergarten with my mother and brother. As we walk into our apartment, there's an air of excitement between them. My brother in particular is skipping and bouncing as he leads me to the living room through the kitchen.

"So? Are you going to show her the surprise?" my mother asks him from the kitchen as she places her grocery bags on the table.

"What is it?" I'm puzzled. I don't recall any special event happening today. "What's going on?"

In the living room, adjacent to the kitchen table, is our family couch. My mother always covers it with a cotton quilt to protect the surface from spills and stains.

Today, as I enter the room, I notice the colour of the cotton quilt is different from the one I saw in the morning.

"Ta-da!" My mother and brother both wave their hands at the couch.

"Wow!" I exclaim, unable to hide my surprise. "We've got a new sofa cover!"

That's the reason for my brother's excitement. Seeing the surprise on my face, he seems satisfied. Together, we dance around the couch celebrating the brand-new sofa cover until my mother calls us both for teatime.

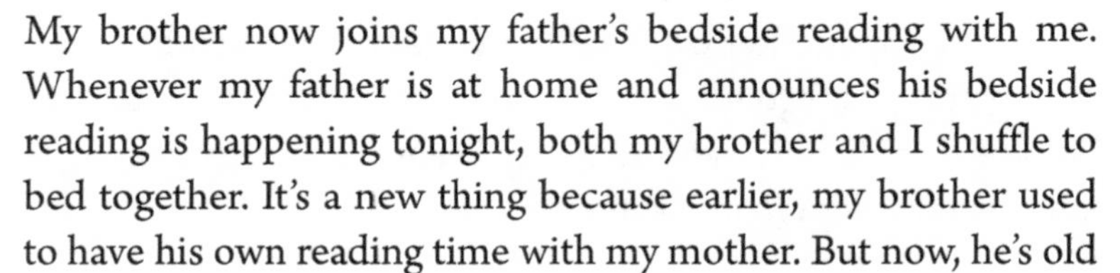

My brother now joins my father's bedside reading with me. Whenever my father is at home and announces his bedside reading is happening tonight, both my brother and I shuffle to bed together. It's a new thing because earlier, my brother used to have his own reading time with my mother. But now, he's old enough to listen to a more grown-up story.

My father is currently reading *Swallows and Amazons* by Arthur Ransome, a story of young children's adventures on boats. When he first started this book, the audience was just me. And I've mostly been a quiet listener, paying attention to the story's details and expressing my thoughts from time to time.

But now, with my brother present, the bedside reading has suddenly become noisy because my brother and I like to discuss the story while our father reads.

There's a character named Peggy in *Swallows and Amazons*. One night, I express something that's always been on my mind. "The name Peggy sounds like a penguin, doesn't it?"

The moment I say that, my brother replies from the other side of our father, "Peggy is a penguin!"

The way he says it is so funny that I burst into laughter. Then my brother says it again, this time louder, while turning in my direction. "Peggy is a penguin!"

This is so much fun that now, whenever the name Peggy comes up, we start chanting, "Peggy is a penguin!" until our father tells us to stop disrupting the story.

House-Hunting

The winter is ending. My parents are talking about buying our first family home. Many of my friends in our community of tiny apartments are also talking about moving. Some of them have already left.

I don't think there's any place better than this paradise we live in, but the idea of house-hunting excites me. I especially enjoy visiting different model homes. Sometimes, I go with my family, and other times, I go with my mother and brother, my two best friends, their mothers and little siblings. They're also planning to move out soon.

Sakura's family are planning to move into a new condo not too far from our current place. One day, we all visit the model home together to see what kind of housing it offers.

After a quick tour, we come back to the reception, where the three mothers have a long conversation with a staff member about the condo, and we six children wander off to the waiting area.

In the middle of the waiting area is a large, elegant dining table. Properly set with plates and cutleries, it's nothing like the one at my home.

"Look!" someone calls out. "We have food here!"

At the centre of the table are plates and bowls full of high-quality fake fruits. They look real from all angles, even the texture.

"Somebody's prepared a feast for us!" I rush to the table, taking a seat. "How lucky we are!"

The six of us sit around the table, helping ourselves to an imaginary feast. We marvel at how real the fruit looks.

"I swear, I've never seen any fake fruits as real as these ones," I tell everyone. "Not even at a department store!"

On our way home, my mother tells us what she's learned about the condo. She sounds like she really likes it. She says the condo is close to my brother's hospital.

I also like it, but for a different reason. I'm thinking about the dining table near the reception. If we can have an elegant table like that one, I'd be happy to move into this condo.

About a week later, my mother takes me and my brother to the same model home exhibition again. This time, we go straight to the reception desk.

While my mother speaks with the staff, my brother and I run to the dining table with the fake fruit. We both remember how fun it was when we came here last time. As we play with the fake fruit, everything we said and did last time comes back to my mind.

We continue playing until my mother finally calls us to go home.

Hinamatsuri

March is here and spring is arriving. Next to the glass doors leading to our balcony is the decoration of traditional Japanese dolls to celebrate our March holiday, *Hinamatsuri*. These are expensive dolls that my grandmother bought us shortly after I was born, and they're usually carefully stored in a box to avoid becoming our toy. Only once a year my mother takes them out to celebrate the holiday.

The dolls recreate an ancient wedding of a noble couple, with the bride and groom and three bridesmaids all dressed in beautiful traditional costumes made of silk. The official wedding scene actually involves more people, my mother once told me, but because our space is limited, my grandmother chose the doll set with only two layers – the couple and the three bridesmaids.

These dolls are so beautiful that I cannot take my eyes off them. I sit in front of them, taking in every detail. Their eyes are so lively that I feel as if they might move at any moment. I look at the bride's beautiful black hair. I'm not allowed to play with her, but I gently run my hand over her long, smooth hair and wonder why she looks so elegant and beautiful. I then observe everybody's hands, which are all shaped as if carrying something.

Watching them closely, I start to feel as if I am part of their world, sitting among them, participating in this ancient wedding.

I hear the sound of the flute and the drum played by the five musicians that my mother told me about.

And I cannot help thinking how magical it is that these dolls have just transformed our tiny living room into the gorgeous world of an ancient wedding scene.

One evening, after an early supper, my mother calls me and my brother to the living room. We've been busy playing in the back room, but hearing our mother's repeated request, we come running to the living room. She's holding her black Pentax film camera in her hands.

"Stand there, sweeties," she says and points behind the *Hinamatsuri* doll set. "I'll take pictures of you and the dolls before I put them away."

There isn't much room between the doll set and the balcony doors, but my brother and I somehow manage to squeeze our small bodies in the narrow gap.

"Great." My mother grins behind her camera. "Now, smile!"

My brother and I smile. But my mother isn't happy.

"Sweeties, where are your smiles?" she asks us as she rolls the film of her camera. "Your *best* smiles?"

To this, my brother quickly responds. He tilts his head, shuts his eyes tightly and smiles from ear to ear. Whenever my mother tells him to smile his best smile, this is what he does. On his right, I broaden my smile.

"There we go! Keep smiling!"

Once the photoshoot is over, my brother and I go back to play. But we don't get to play for long. Shortly after my father comes home, my mother and brother leave for the large hospital where my brother will be having his heart operation in a few days.

Yamaha Music Showcase and Muscat Grape Chewing Gum

On March 9th, the annual showcase of my Yamaha music school takes place in the concert hall outside of the city centre. I'm wearing the same outfit as last year, and the only difference this year is that two of my family members are missing: my mother and brother. Tomorrow is the day of my brother's major heart surgery, and they're staying at the large hospital. But my father and grandmother are here with me.

Several Electones are placed on the stage along with microphones and colourful cubes. During the stage rehearsal, our teacher tells us to sit on the cubes facing the audience whenever we're not performing.

The showcase begins, and we perform the pieces we've practiced over the past months. There are songs we sing all together, then there are Electone performances done in smaller groups. I'm in the first group to perform, and once I finish playing, I sit down on one of the colourful cubes next to one of the Electones. Sakura sits on the cube next to me.

It's so funny to look at the audience from the stage. When I share that with Sakura, she agrees, giggling. "Why are we sitting on the stage staring at them?"

"So weird!"

"Are they watching us?"

"Sitting on the cubes, doing nothing?"

We burst into laughter. Once we start laughing, there's no stopping it. We try and fail at hiding our hysterical giggles throughout the other group's performance.

Once all the performances are done, everybody receives a bouquet and a bag of goodies as a souvenir, and we all walk to a large room for the group photo.

After the showcase event, my father, grandmother and I head over to the hospital to meet my mother and brother. Still in my stage costume, holding the bouquet and the bag of goodies, I follow my father and grandmother down the familiar corridor of the hospital, onto the elevator.

My mother and brother are waiting for us in the hallway. The moment the elevator door opens, my brother shoots to his feet and rushes to us. To my surprise, my aunt and my paternal grandmother are also there.

I'm so eager to show my brother the things I got at the showcase. Together, we open the paper bag and take out Mickey Mouse themed pencils, eraser and plastic folders.

Suddenly, my brother grabs one of the folders and runs off. I immediately go after him. The next moment, we're running around the elevator hall chasing each other, laughing like crazy.

"Stop it, both of you." My father frowns. "You're making too much noise. This is a hospital, not your home!"

My brother and I collapse on the bench, laughing and sweating from the exercise. While we're having such a fun time, it would be even nicer to have something to snack on.

"Oh, I wish I'd brought my Muscat grape gum with me!" I exclaim.

"I have mine," says my brother next to me.

"Where?"

"In my room."

"Let's go get it!"

We both stand up and dash through the corridor heading to my brother's room. As we run at our top speed, it strikes me how my little brother is no longer a toddler and feels more like an equal companion to me. He's turning three in just a few months.

Once in the room, my brother goes to his bed, opens his blue shoulder bag hanging on the bedpost, and takes out a green package of Muscat grape chewing gum. He moves around the room with such ease and confidence, it's as if he's always lived here.

When my brother hands me the package, I realize it's still sealed.

"Wow, a brand-new package. Hurray!"

I jump with delight, and my brother follows my lead as he always does. When I tell him that thanks to him, we can enjoy the gum, his face glows with pride.

Together, we run back to the bench in the elevator hall where we savour the chewing gum. It's just another ordinary day in which I play and share my favourite snack with my little brother.

Part 4

Departure

The Morning

March 10th. Early in the morning, I visit my brother in his hospital room with my father, grandmothers and aunt. It's the same room where my brother and I came to pick up his gum yesterday. But now, with many people bustling in and out, I barely recognize the place.

On the TV next to my brother's bed, his favourite program "Play in English!" is playing. But my brother is barely paying attention. He's crying badly, so unlike him, and no matter what the adults around him say or do to cheer him up, he cries harder.

"Poor kid," someone says. "With all that's going on around him, he doesn't feel like himself."

So many adults – my parents and relatives, joined by nurses – surround my brother I can hardly see him. Peeking through the wall of adults, I fight my frustration. *Why can't I go closer?*

The nurse does something to my brother that makes his cry even worse. *Why can't I go closer*? I should be the one next to him. My brother is never sad when I'm with him because I know how to make him laugh! But from this far, I cannot reach him or talk to him. I don't think he even sees me.

While my brother continues to have a tantrum, my father suddenly remembers he needs to get something from the hospital's kiosk. Because everybody is swarming my brother and I'm bored on my own, I decide to accompany my father.

"Come back quick," calls out my mother as we leave the room, a sense of urgency filling her voice. "Come back before he goes."

As soon as we leave the room, however, the day feels like any other day. Walking down the corridor with my father, the situation reminds me of our weekend shopping.

I'm only accompanying my father, but at the kiosk, a few Sailor Moon toys catch my eye. One of them is a plastic Sailor Moon doll that's also a piggy-bank. My father tells me I can pick one, but I cannot decide which one I want.

"Hurry up," says my father after a while. "Your brother is leaving for the operation. We need to be there before he goes."

"Why?" I ask him lazily. "It's not a big deal." *It's not a big deal because I'll see him again when the surgery is over.*

My brother was born with heart disease, and he's gone through many operations. Whenever he has a surgery, I have to wait alone, possibly for weeks, before I can see him again. But I'll be all right. Because I know when he comes back, he'll be happy again, and we can play together.

Finally, I choose the plastic Sailor Moon doll, and my father and I run back to my brother's floor. When we get there, however, we find everybody standing in the hallway. My mother tells us that my brother has just left.

"What's taken you so long?" she asks us. Her eyes are red and puffy, her voice more sad than angry. "Your brother went off with his blue shoulder bag, waving his hand and looking like a big boy."

As my mother explains, an image takes form in my mind. My brother is walking down a red corridor, wearing his bag and waving.

"I was choosing my toy," I answer. And I think I see a hint of sadness in my mother's eyes, even though she doesn't say anything further.

My parents, my two grandmothers, my aunt and I go out for lunch at a restaurant inside the hospital. As I sit and eat, I remember the dinner from last night when my brother and I ran around the restaurant with the Mickey Mouse pencils and folders like two mad people.

Now, it's so quiet. The adults are also less talkative. At the end of the meal, my mother lets me order a melon soda with ice cream for dessert. The bright red cherry on top of the ice cream is such a contrast to the somber air in the room.

After lunch, my parents stay at the hospital, and I go back home with my maternal grandmother.

The Evening

It's a quiet evening at home. I eat dinner, watch my regular TV programs, play with my dolls, and go to sleep after taking a bath.

I sleep with my grandmother in the back room. When she prepares her futon next to mine, it's just like those days when I stayed at her place by myself. Only this time, *she's* at *my* home.

Just as I lie down and pull up my blanket, my grandmother opens her mouth. "I just hope everything goes well for your brother." She sounds as if she's making a wish. "That his operation will be successful."

"Of course it will be, Grandma. How can it not?" I'm puzzled. This isn't his first surgery. She must know that.

My grandmother doesn't seem to go to sleep tonight. After wishing me a good night, she stays up, sitting on her futon. Then I hear her murmur something. When I peek through my half-closed eyes, her eyes are closed and her hands are folded. She's praying. *But why?* That's my last thought before falling asleep.

The News

I wake up from a wonderful sleep with happy dreams. When my eyes open, morning has already arrived. Two faces hover above me. My mother's and father's. They're smiling, though awkward smiles. How long have they been here? Have they been waiting for me? Their eyes search mine as I slowly become conscious.

And then I remember everything.

"How did it go?" Words burst out of my mouth. "How was the surgery?"

There's a pause. It's my mother who opens her mouth. "Your brother did so well..." she starts, then her voice cracks. "But he didn't make it."

"Didn't make it?" I repeat blankly. My eyes search both my parents' faces for further explanations. But the only thing I find is their smiles and red eyes.

"*Didn't make it?*" I jump out of my blanket. "Where is he?"

"In the living room."

I dash to our tiny living room, through the open sliding door. There on the floor, in front of our family couch, lies my little brother on the futon he used to use for his daily nap until recently.

He looks almost as if he were asleep. But something tells me that he's not.

I hear somebody's wail in the room. It takes a moment for me to realize that the sound actually comes from me.

My mother puts me on her lap, and I bury my face in her shoulder. The loud sob doesn't seem to end. I cry until my face becomes puffy, and my throat is too hoarse to produce any more sound.

Then, just as abruptly as it started, my crying stops. I look at my brother's face and notice something fluffy fitted in his mouth.

"What's this?"

"I'm told it's cotton."

"What's it for?"

"I'm not sure."

I touch my brother's face. It's cold.

"He's cold."

"He was still warm when we brought him home from the hospital."

My mother then tells me how my brother came home earlier this morning.

A picture takes form in my mind. My mother's driving back on the familiar road with my father in the passenger seat and my brother lying on the back seat. In the early morning light, the car drives down the winding road by the rocky wall, across the river, passing the art gallery and the post office, and back to our apartment. My brother was still warm then.

How is it possible that his body has turned this cold so quickly? I wonder if in those few hours my brother has really gone somewhere for good. And I wish I'd been there with him.

Goodbyes

The day gets busy. Upon the news of my brother's passing, many people visit our tiny home. They're our friends and neighbours. My relatives also arrive from far-away cities.

As more people come to my home, the shock that swallowed me earlier is replaced by a sense of wonder and excitement. My family have never had so many guests at once before. I hide in the back room watching my parents speak with the guests in the living room.

Before noon, my aunt takes me to the railway station. Her three daughters are arriving by train, and we're going to pick them up.

As we come out of one of the buildings near the station onto the pedestrian deck, suddenly, my aunt sways her hips from side to side like a fish – a funny gesture she often does to make me and my brother laugh. A giggle escapes me. My first laugh of the day. Hearing my laugh, my aunt does the move again.

I almost forget why we're here at the station and why all my cousins are travelling so far today. But the absence of a smile on my aunt's face and her urgent tone when speaking with her daughters remind me of all the people at home. Their tears. And my brother lying still in our living room.

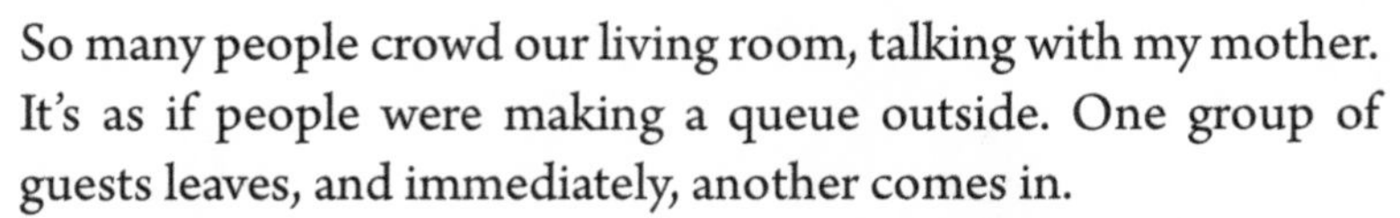

So many people crowd our living room, talking with my mother. It's as if people were making a queue outside. One group of guests leaves, and immediately, another comes in.

I'm in the back room playing with my older cousins. For some reason, I play with a toy that I thought I graduated from a long time ago. A yellow plastic spiral inside a transparent cylinder. I drop colourful balls from the top and watch them fall down the spiral one after another, making a chiming sound at the end. There's no meaning to it, but it's something to keep me busy and the muffled voices in the next room a distant sound.

In the early afternoon, Sakura and Karen visit my home with their mothers and little siblings.

My heart leaps with joy upon seeing their familiar faces. I haven't realized how disoriented I feel until now. How my home hasn't felt like home at all. Now, with their arrival, this place finally feels right again. The sense of relief is so huge that I even start skipping like I normally do in their presence.

But today, there are no smiles on their faces. They're all quiet – even Karen's little sister and Sakura's little brother – as they slowly enter our living room, sitting down next to my brother.

More surprise than sadness fills their features. I try talking to my friends, but it's as if they've forgotten how to speak. Their eyes are fixed on my brother, who remains motionless. Normally, he'd be the first person to welcome them at the door.

My mother tells them about how he came home earlier that day. Everybody listens without making any sound.

Then I hear a rustling sound.

"Here," Karen's little sister holds out something in her hand. It's a fruit lollipop like we always eat on our way back home from music school. She and my brother normally enjoy several of them during our music class while they roam around the classroom using their sibling privilege.

A small laugh leaves Karen's mother. "You want to give it to him?"

As she places the lollipop next to my brother's pillow, it hits me that this is the first time somebody has given anything to my brother today. Many have brought flowers and gifts, but they were for my parents, not for my brother.

My gaze lingers on the familiar lollipop next to my brother's face. On this abnormal day, this candy reminds me of our normal days. Those fun ordinary days we've always had together.

Sometime in the afternoon, another familiar face visits my home. The lady from the tofu shop across the street – the person who always waves at us from her shopfront whenever she finds me or my brother by the open window of our back room.

Out of awkwardness, I don't greet the lady, but I watch her from the back room. Dressed in black, she's brought flowers with her. She speaks eagerly with my mother, her handkerchief pressed to her eyes every now and then.

I'm surprised that she's here, and even more surprised that she's crying. We're just acquaintances, not friends. Or at least, that's what I thought. Somebody we greet from afar – across the street, through a window. But here she is, talking to my mother about my brother with tears in her eyes.

In the late afternoon, people in black suits come over and put my brother in a wooden box. My mother asks the men what is allowed in the box, and after some back and forth, a few toy buses and my brother's favourite Pooh bear plush are placed next to my brother's body along with white lilies.

Then I'm told that we're heading somewhere else. When I come out of my apartment block, a large, box-shaped car is waiting for us.

"Aren't we going by our car?" Surprise flickers through me.

"No." My mother's answer is minimum. "Get in."

Since I've never travelled in such a spacious car, I get excited as I sit next to my father. My mother sits across from us, next to the wooden box that has my brother in it.

The comfortable ride lasts only a brief time. We're somewhere in the city centre. The men in suits take out the wooden box, and I follow my parents into the building in front of us. Somebody tells me that this is a funeral home. Not that I know what it means.

The room is packed with men and women in black suits and dresses. Some of their faces I don't know, but many are familiar. My relatives. My friends and their families. My kindergarten teachers. They're all here in this one room.

I sit next to my parents in the front row. The wooden box carrying my brother's body is right in front of us surrounded by countless white flowers. There's a large picture of my brother placed above the wooden box.

I know this picture. It was taken last autumn on the day we were supposed to visit my paternal grandmother but had to cancel the plan because I got sick.

That day, most of the pictures my mother took captured me and my brother together, but she also took some solo pictures of us. This picture in front of us shows my brother sitting in his favourite place – the little space on the hilltop of our community where the out-of-service local buses come to spend their down time. Wearing his signature red jacket, he's smiling toward his right, both of his hands folded as if holding his toy buses.

The ceremony begins and people come and speak at the microphone, talking about memories of my brother. The air is heavy and sorrowful.

Suddenly, familiar music plays from the speaker. It's Pachelbel's "Canon," my brother's nap music.

"He used to listen to this music every day when he took a daily nap," somebody explains through the microphone, and I hear people sob.

This is strange. I shift my body in my chair. It all feels strange to hear these people speak of my brother in the past tense. He's here. Inside that wooden box over there.

There's also nothing sad about this music. It's actually a funny story. Before he stopped taking his daily nap, my brother used to refuse to sleep whenever this music started playing. And my mother and I had to pretend to sleep in order to get my brother's attention. Thinking about that now makes me want to laugh.

But I remain quiet. I keep looking around instead, observing the people, my brother's picture, and everything else in the room. I cannot help thinking that all of this feels strange.

Suddenly, my mother pokes me. The facilitator is now introducing my parents and me to the attendees in the room. We're each called by our name and our relationship to my brother. I'm introduced as his big sister. My face breaks into a smile of pride as I stand next to my parents and take a bow.

Then, the ceremony comes to an end. It's time for a feast.

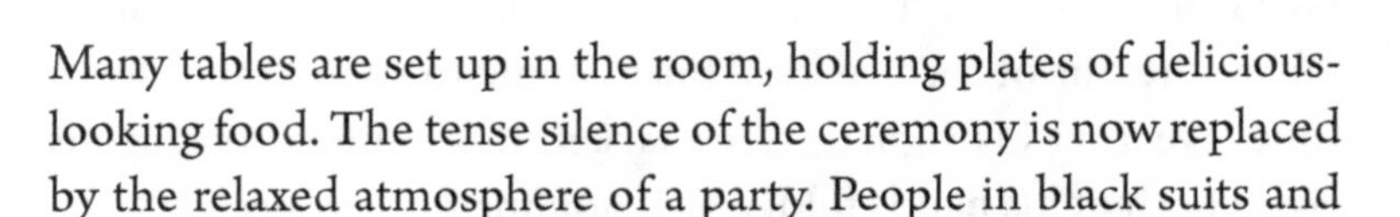

Many tables are set up in the room, holding plates of delicious-looking food. The tense silence of the ceremony is now replaced by the relaxed atmosphere of a party. People in black suits and dresses huddle around the tables, and once a toast is made, their chattering voices quickly fill the room.

No longer required to sit still, I immediately look for my best friends, Sakura and Karen, and once we're united, we play together, picking food from different tables. It feels like a long time has passed since we last played together at our music event, even though that was only a few days ago.

When I'm at one table grabbing some food, a familiar voice speaks to me. It's my kindergarten's head teacher. But today, she isn't wearing jeans and a colourful shirt. She's wearing a black dress like everyone else.

"It's going to be lonely for you without him," she says, holding a glass of yellow liquid in her hand. Her cheeks are pink, and I wonder if it's one of those drinks that are forbidden to us children. "You're going to miss him."

Up until now, my mind has been busy with food and my friends, but something about the way she says it snags my attention. I look at her face more carefully. She's smiling, but there's a sheen of tears in her eyes.

"Maybe," I reply.

To this, my teacher says nothing. She smiles at me once again, and we talk about something else.

But my mind stays with what she's just said. *You're going to miss him.* Something about it feels important. I cannot yet put my finger on it, but I decide to think about it later, perhaps tomorrow.

I go back to playing with my friends.

Later that evening, Karen and her family stay with us until after everybody else goes home. While the adults are talking, I take out one toy I brought with me from home. The plastic Sailor Moon doll that my father bought me at the hospital kiosk.

"Let's play with this!" The room might have been designed for a serious ceremony, but for us, it's just another place to have fun. "I'm going to hide this toy somewhere in this room, so your task is to find it!"

We take turns hiding and finding the toy. Karen's little sister also joins us. When it's her turn to find the toy, Karen and I decide to hide it under the table on which my brother's wooden box is laid. The heavy white cloth covering the table reaches the floor, creating a perfect spot for the toy to disappear.

Karen's sister looks for the toy, but cannot find it.

"Oh, we've found such a genius place to hide it!" Karen and I skip around the room, teasing her. "Can you find it, oh, can you find it?"

After a while, I give her a hint. "It's near my brother!"

So, she starts rummaging around all the flowers and serious decorations that surround my brother's wooden box, and Karen and I become even more excited. So much so that we do cartwheels on the floor. That's when our parents come over to grab us.

"Enough, girls," warn our fathers. "That's enough! For goodness' sake, this is a funeral home! You're being too noisy!"

But we're still laughing like mad people, sweating from our exercise. I'm sure my brother would be thrilled to join us if he could.

"We're going home," says Karen's father. "You all need to calm down."

Karen and I reveal to her sister where we hid the toy. "It was a perfect place, wasn't it?"

When it's finally time for Karen's family to go home, I follow them to the elevator in the back of the room. As I wave goodbye, it feels just like the end of any other day. Laughing and sweating. Even the room, which held a serious atmosphere earlier, now feels like an extension of our home. And the news of my brother's passing feels like a distant dream.

My family and relatives sleep in the small room adjacent to the one where my brother's funeral ceremony took place. I'm told this is customary when somebody in your family passes away. To me, however, sleeping here feels only natural because I know my brother is asleep in the next room. Unless we take him back home, we should also stay here.

Sleeping in this room with everybody else reminds me of the time when we took a family trip to a hot spring resort. Still sweating from the blast I've just had with my friends, I lie down on my futon with my new Sailor Moon doll.

The next morning, many people come and fill the room once again. Just when I wonder if we're going to do the long ceremony all over again, my parents, relatives and I are guided downstairs, then outside, by the funeral home staff. A minibus is waiting for us in front of the building.

"Hop inside," somebody calls out, and I do as I'm told, delighted to have another ride in a large vehicle. In fact, I'm so happy to be free from the ceremonies and be on the move that as soon as I take a window seat next to my father, I become chatty.

Until my mother's urgent voice reaches me. "Look outside."

The moment I follow her gaze and look out the window, my breath snags in disbelief. So many people. So many people in black are standing on the staircase in front of the building's entrance. The entire space is packed with people.

As my eyes scan the crowd, I spot Sakura and Karen and their families among them. I realize that all these people are our guests who came to my brother's funeral yesterday.

The minibus starts to move, and my parents tell me to take a bow. But I'm unable to look away from my friends, who are staring in this direction. From their puzzled expressions, I can tell they're as clueless as I am about this whole event.

As the minibus picks up speed and the people on the staircase wave their hands at us, I hold on to my friends' familiar faces as if they were the only thing I can count on in this world.

After a long drive, we get off in front of a strange building. Yet another building I've never been to.

My brother is once again carried out from the vehicle in the wooden box. By now, I've grown used to seeing him inside the box. *But when are we going home?* This is what I'm starting to wonder. Because, surely we cannot continue travelling like this forever, can we?

We're not taken to any room this time. The box that carries my brother's body is placed on a heavy-looking metal cart, and we all gather in the hallway. People grow tearful once again. Somebody has opened the tiny window of the wooden box, revealing my brother's sleeping face.

"Sweetie, remember your brother's face," says my mother. Her face is distorted from her effort not to break into tears. "Have a good look at him. You're going to remember his face."

I don't understand why my mother is suddenly being so dramatic. Of course I remember his face. I see him every day.

But something about the way my mother speaks to me urges me to listen.

I look at my brother's face – that familiar face I've seen every day since the day he joined our family. This is my little brother who's always chased me around, who's stubbornly refused to take a nap, who's sometimes hit me during our fights, who's run around with my friend's sister at our weekly music lessons, who's crazy about buses and has a habit of watching buses wherever possible. And I'm his big sister.

My mother asks me if I've taken a good look, and I nod.

The tiny window of the wooden box is closed, and the metal cart is pushed into a space that reminds me of the parking tower next to my music school.

At the music school, my mother drives our car into the towering building. Once she comes out, the metal door closes, swallowing the car behind it. Then we hear the machine operate the huge wheel inside the windowless tower, shuffling all the cars inside it.

Here, when the cart with my brother's box is secured in place, a thick metal door closes, swallowing the cart and the wooden box behind it. I vaguely wonder what's going to happen inside, but the thought is cut off when the staff guides us away from the hallway. We're led to some sort of waiting room. Tea and snacks are served, and I immediately help myself.

People are talking about my brother. My mother's telling somebody how my toddler brother used to sing a very difficult song that played at the end of each Sailor Moon episode. "He had no idea what he was singing about," she laughs with glistening eyes. "The content was too mature for him. But he sang anyway, and he sang well."

The time passes like that, and finally, we're called back to the hallway.

In front of us, the heavy metal door opens, and the cart comes into sight as the staff pulls it out. But there's no wooden box resting on it.

"Where is the ... ?"

My words trail off. Where there used to be a wooden box a while ago, something else now lies. Something very white. It takes a moment for me to realize that these are bones. So many bones.

Upon the staff's signal, everybody huddles over the metal cart, over the white bones.

As I watch the bones closely, totally lost and filled with wonder, somebody hands me a pair of chopsticks. It's my mother.

"Pick up the bones with your chopsticks and put them in here." She points at the little porcelain pot placed on the cart. When I reach for one of the many bone pieces, she reminds me. "Be gentle. This is your brother."

I'm not sure if I really get it. That my brother's body has been turned into these many pieces of bones. What's happened in that dark place behind the metal door? I mean, how can this be?

I'm too shocked to be able to even think about it. I just follow what others around me do. I pick up the bones one by one and place them into the tiny pot.

Prayer

The day after the funeral, I go to kindergarten as usual. It feels strangely normal to be in the classroom surrounded by familiar faces after the eventful weekend. The school year is about to end, making this one of the last days I spend with my teacher and classmates.

Once everybody comes in, teacher Mina calls us for the morning meeting. We all sit on the floor in a semicircle, facing her.

"Today, we have sad news," she begins, and I immediately know what's coming next. "Maiko's little brother has passed away."

The room falls silent. Among my kindergarten friends, only a handful came to the funeral. Those from our community of apartments, who'd known my brother well. Not all of my classmates have yet heard the news.

"We've all met him," teacher Mina continues. "He always came here with his mother to pick up Maiko. Last weekend, he had a difficult heart surgery, and to our great sadness, he passed away."

Nobody makes any sound.

"He's now resting in Heaven. So, let's offer him our prayer so that he will know we're thinking of him."

With that, she starts the prayer. It begins just like any other prayer we have every day at kindergarten. Only her tone is sorrowful and her voice is quiet.

At the end of the short prayer, my teacher says my brother's name, and I feel a surge of pride that his name is now known to everybody in this room. *If he were here,* I think to myself, *he'd be so happy right now*. But he's not here. And so I try even harder to remember this special prayer in my heart on his behalf.

Part 5

Grief and Treasure

(April 1996 -)

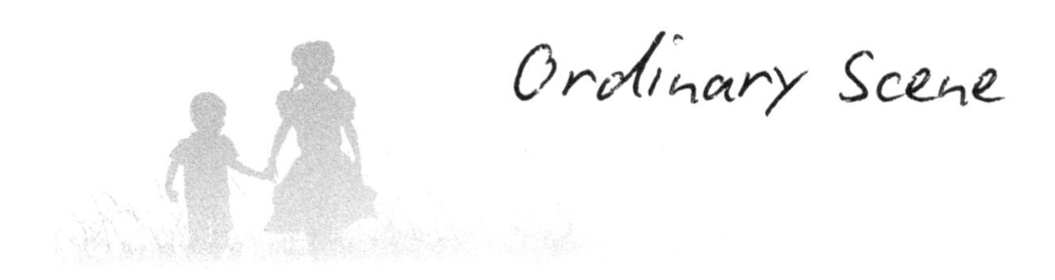

Ordinary Scene

One morning in early April, about a month after my brother's funeral. I stand in front of my apartment block with my two best friends, Sakura and Karen. Today is the first day of the new school year, our senior year at kindergarten, and the three of us are dressed in prettier clothes than usual. I'm wearing my favourite red polka-dot skirt.

The air is charged with excitement for the new school day as the pale pink petals of the cherry blossoms shower upon us. Under the bright blue sky, we stand and chat. Which class will we be in? Who'll be our new teacher?

Suddenly, my mother comes running with her black film camera in her hands.

"Girls, come here!" she calls out with a big smile on her face. "I'm going to take a picture of you three. How pretty you all look!"

Still busy with chatting, we're slow to respond.

"Girls," says my mother again, this time with more force. "Please stand there while I take a picture of you!"

I don't understand why my mother is obsessed with taking photos when we're having such a fun time. But the three of us finally line up facing the camera. Only I cannot stop talking and laughing.

"Stop chatting and look here!" This time, my mother specifically addresses me. "Now!"

I reluctantly stop talking and turn toward the camera. But there's no way I'm smiling after being picked on like that. Moreover, next to my two best friends!

"Sweetie!" my mother shouts at me as she rolls the film. "Smile, please!"

As soon as the photoshoot is over, my mother rushes to me.

"Why didn't you smile?" she asks, her tone more of an accusation than a question. "You were the only one who wasn't smiling!"

In late April, I'm sitting with Sakura and Karen in the playground. Our playhouse activity has come to a halt, and currently we're just sitting, dangling our legs in the spring breeze.

"She says she feels sorry for Maiko." One of my friends' voices grabs my attention. "She even cried when we chatted."

"That's not surprising," the other voice responds quietly. "I know many friends who feel the same way."

"But my other classmate said something else," the first one continues. "She told me that she doesn't feel any pity. She said she isn't sorry at all!"

"Really?"

I know which girls they're talking about. I haven't played with either of them much, so I don't know them well. But still, it's a shock to hear that somebody can feel no sympathy for my brother's passing. I mean, why does anybody say they're not sorry at all?

"That's awful," says the other friend after a while. "I think that's mean."

"Me too. I told her 'You don't know what you're talking about. Her brother passed away.'"

"And?"

"She just shrugged."

I remain silent. For some reason, I feel detached from this whole conversation. I guess people can feel whatever they want. But what I know for sure is that this girl wouldn't have said whatever she did if it'd been her brother who died.

"Don't be so angry." I finally open my mouth. "She just doesn't get it. Plus, she didn't really know my brother. So, she cannot feel sorry."

"We know your brother," my friends say in chorus. "He's so sweet. The sweetest!"

"That's true." A smile returns to my face.

"We'll always remember him. And we're always here for you."

The way they say it makes whatever other people say about my brother seem so small and unimportant. I smile, and the three of us go back to our play.

Absence

One day shortly after the funeral, while playing at home, I come across the familiar package of Muscat grape chewing gum. It's the one my brother and I opened the evening before his surgery. I cannot believe I didn't return it to him that night. It was *his* package, not mine.

There are still several pieces of gum remaining in the package, and without much thought, I open one and throw it into my mouth.

As the familiar sweet flavour spreads on my tongue, the memory of that day comes back to me. I remember how my brother and I dashed through the corridor in excitement, how he took the green package from his shoulder bag hung on his bedpost, and how we both made a toast before eating the chewing gum, while sitting in the elevator hall.

I cannot believe he's gone. How can he be gone? Maybe he's still somewhere.

I think about my brother's whereabouts as I slowly chew on my gum in the empty back room.

It's a weekend morning. In the living room, I sit on one half of my mother's lap. The other half is kept for my brother.

From time to time, I look at the sliding door separating this room from the back room, searching for my brother's familiar figure. "It's weird he's not here," I tell my mother. "I can almost see him standing there!"

"So can I," she replies, her gaze also lingering on the door. "With his sleepy face and messy hair."

"Yes, his sleepy face and messy hair."

We then look at each other and laugh. But the laugh doesn't last for long. My mother's eyes have glistened, and she quickly takes off her glasses to wipe away her tears.

Though my brother's gone, my mother keeps his belongings exactly where they used to be. His clothes, his books, his plates, and even his medical supplies. Only his toy buses and a few of his other favourite toys have been moved to my brother's altar.

Everything that has anything to do with my brother carries a special importance to my mother. Even his drawing of the Kind Sun on the back-room wall, that once caused a great scandal in the house, is now an object of her adoration and protection. When a relative or a family friend visits us, my mother often takes them to the back room and shows them my brother's work.

I cannot help thinking back on the day when we made those drawings and how my mother was upset with us. Now, my brother's Kind Sun is my mother's anchor.

At bedtime, my father reads me *Swallows and Amazons*. We've now past the midpoint, and the story is slowly moving toward the climax. But I cannot shake off the feeling that something is missing.

Whenever the character Peggy's name is mentioned, I shout, "Peggy is a penguin!" like I've grown used to doing over the past months. The only difference now is that there's nobody to respond to this silly joke. No more cheeky smile peeking from my father's other side. No more chaos disturbing the story's progress.

"It's strange," I tell my father one day. "Why is it so quiet? I wish my brother was here! He'd say 'Peggy is a penguin' so many times! That was so fun!"

One day, we're eating dinner when my father says he had a nightmare last night.

"What nightmare?" I ask, worried what kind of monster showed up in the dream.

"Your brother was there."

"What?"

"He was smiling and laughing next to me."

"*What?*" My voice is raised. "Daddy, that's a happy dream! I'm so jealous! Oh, I hope he'll come to my dream, too!" I exclaim with such seriousness that a confused laugh escapes my father.

"It might be a happy dream for you, but not for me."

"But WHY, Daddy?"

My father exchanges a look with my mother and no one says any more about that topic. Only I'm wondering how I can see my brother more often in my dreams.

Bubbles

Some time in May, Sakura, Karen and I are talking about my brother. They're one of the few people outside of my family who still talk about him as if he truly mattered in their lives.

"He was so sweet," we say to each other, recalling the time when we all used to play together in one of our apartments. "Wish he was still here!"

Suddenly, a brilliant idea occurs to me.

"When my brother was staying at hospital, he had a soap bar he used every day. And Mommy still has it. Why don't we make bubbles out of it?"

Some time ago, we learned how to make bubble solution out of a soap bar at kindergarten.

"That's a great idea." My friends' faces are also lit up. "Let's do it!"

My mother is surprised when the three of us barge into the tiny kitchen of my apartment and express our keen desire to make bubble solution out of my brother's soap bar.

In any other situation, she would've said no. Everything related to my brother is her treasure and not to be wasted. But our faces are bright with anticipation, and our intent is genuine. My mother gives us permission to use my brother's soap bar to make the bubble solution.

We grate the soap bar with a knife, putting the pieces into three empty jam jars, then mix them well with water. The solution is ready. My mother gives us plastic straws to blow the bubbles. Now, all we need to do is to find a good place outside to try out our bubble solution.

After walking around the square playground for some time, we decide on the street right outside the playground next to the community's entrance. That's the most spacious area with fewer people to disturb us.

The three of us spread out, each holding a jar of bubble solution. I place mine on the road to free up my hands as I start blowing. The solution easily produces many small bubbles out of our straws.

"My brother's bubble solution is amazing!" My face breaks into a wide grin. "It's magical!"

It doesn't take long before I get lost in the experience and lose attention to my surroundings.

Suddenly, a voice calls out. "Watch out, a car is coming!"

When I look up, the car is already in front of us. Panicked, I run to the side, forgetting about everything else.

As the car goes by, one of its tires knocks over a jar, spilling all of its contents. That's when I realize I've left my jar on the street. It was my bubble solution that spilled.

"My bubbles!!" I cry out, dashing to my jar as soon as the car is gone. But it's too late. Not a drop remains. I've wasted it all. And it was a very special bubble solution. My brother's bubble solution…

I do what I normally don't do in front of my friends: I break into sobs. It's so unfair that my bubble solution is all gone. I don't know what to do now.

As I cry, I slowly become aware of my friends standing several feet away from me, whispering something to each other.

Do they think it's silly of me to cry over such a small thing? That's what my mother tells me whenever I throw a tantrum.

A few moments later, they finish their secret talk and approach me. "You can have ours," they tell me, holding out their jars.

"Really?" I'm so surprised I stop crying.

Sakura and Karen both pour some from their jars into mine until all three jars have an equal amount of solution in them. We then blow bubbles again. This time, away from the street.

"No more cars, no more spilling!" we chant. "Watch out for our special bubbles!"

We continue blowing the bubbles until all the liquid is gone. There's not a single trace of tears on my face when we finish playing.

Kindergarten Summer Camp

In July, my kindergarten hosts an overnight trip for all the kids in my year to a small village on the foot of Mt. Zao, located a few hours drive to the south from our town.

We've all looked forward to this day for so long. Our brilliant teachers have arranged this trip in a way that makes us feel as if we were part of an adventure story. They've been reading the story every day since the beginning of the school year, and now, we're finally going into the world where these characters live.

On the day of the trip, I leave home with a red Snoopy backpack packed with clothes, a water bottle and snacks. Sakura and Karen are also with me. This is the first time I will stay overnight with them, and that makes this trip even more special.

Once at the hostel, we change and walk out into the surrounding forest for our first activity. Our teachers have created a scavenger hunt based on that adventure story! Our mission, we're told, is to answer questions and collect requested items along the way. By the time we reach the end of the hunt, I'm totally convinced that the story has come true in my real life.

In the evening, after dinner, we sit around the campfire and sing songs and dance – our month-long practice coming to fruition. I'm enthralled by the magnificent view of the burning fire, the smoky scent that fills the air, and the powerful togetherness as we sing and dance under the starry sky.

After the long evening, we go back to the hostel to sleep. While we were gone, somebody prepared futons for us. These futons cover the floors of the two large rooms allotted to us. Some of us throw pillows, but before long, the room becomes silent as we all drift off to sleep, taken out by the exhaustion of the adventurous day.

Sometime in early morning, I wake up to a soft sound. It must be close to dawn. I can see a faint light seeping through the window. Two teachers are talking behind me in whisper, reflecting on yesterday's events and preparing for the day that's about to start.

For a few moments, I try to listen to their conversation, but their presence is so comforting that my eyes drift closed again. The next time they open, the sun has risen, and many of us are moving about, ready to start our second day of adventure.

"There's a bug in your eye!" My teacher's concerned eyes meet mine. I've just come out of the breakfast room and greeted my teacher and a group of friends walking with her.

"Yes, she's right!" one of my friends exclaims in surprise. "There *is* a bug in your eye!"

The news doesn't quite hit me because I cannot picture a bug crawling in my eye. That's weird.

"But how did it end up in her eye?" Somebody verbalizes my question.

"We don't know," replies my teacher without taking her eyes off me. "It could've been last night when we were at the campfire. In any case, we must notify our head teacher."

The thing quickly becomes big. I'm first taken to our head teacher, then to the headmaster, who joined us last night. After a brief discussion, it's decided that the headmaster will drive me to the nearest hospital.

"I'm sorry, but you'll have to miss today's activity for now."

"How much?" I cannot hide my concern, not for my eye but for having to miss today's activity.

"Hopefully not much. But we must take you to the hospital before the bug can go farther into your eye. That's the top priority."

With that, the headmaster and I leave the rest behind and hop onto his tiny black car. We drive down the mountain towards the nearby town. All the while, I sit quietly in the front passenger seat, feeling sad to be separated from my friends.

The headmaster is a kind person, and he tries to cheer me up by talking, though without much success. Since I've never personally interacted with him before, I'm being cautious, choosing to focus my attention on the huge round street lights outside than to engage in the conversation.

Once at the hospital, while waiting for my turn, the kind headmaster offers to buy me a cold drink from the vending machine. But I firmly refuse, following the advice I've learned somewhere which said not to allow a stranger to treat you.

When my turn finally arrives, the doctor takes a quick look at my eyes.

"Oh, that's the one." That's all I hear before he picks up a pair of tweezers and plunges them to the edge of my eye. Before I can feel any fear or panic, the tweezers leave my eye.

"There you go. The bug is gone! It's good that you came here right away," the doctor tells us. "The bug hasn't really gone into your eye yet. That's why it was easy to remove it."

Relieved that there's no more bug in my eye, the headmaster and I hop back onto his black car. The only sad part is that I've had to miss the whole morning activity. When the headmaster called the rest of the group, he was told that they'd just finished their final activity and were now on the way back to kindergarten.

"Where did they go?" Even though I've missed it, I cannot help asking about the place.

"They went to a place called the House of Birds. You can see many different birds there."

I feel so jealous of others that I almost make a grumpy face, but I somehow manage not to. The headmaster has been so kind to help me. It would be rude to show my disappointment in front of him.

On the way back, the headmaster and I start chatting. My stranger syndrome has dissolved during the hospital adventure, and there's now a friendly feeling between us. We talk about the passing scenery and my adventure from yesterday, and before long, we find the yellow kindergarten bus carrying my friends and teachers, and it's time for me to rejoin the others.

The kindergarten bus drops me and some of my friends at the square playground at our community. The parents have been waiting, and our teachers go to each of them, telling them about the trip and our individual highlights from the adventure.

After the brief festivity, the teachers depart on the kindergarten bus, and we also disperse, each heading to their home. I wave at Sakura and Karen before following my mother to our apartment right behind the playground.

Nobody else is at home. Once I take off my backpack, my mother prepares a futon in the back room so that I can take a nap. There's no more playing with friends today. I'll rest, then have dinner, most likely.

As I lie down and get comfortable under my blanket, however, I struggle to fall asleep. It's too quiet. And it feels too lonely.

When I shut my eyes, a memory from early this morning replays in my mind. How I lay among my friends and how my teachers were chatting behind me. Then the campfire last night. How we sang and danced around the fire together under the starry sky. And this morning's bug incident and how the headmaster and I drove to the hospital together. After that, how I rejoined others in the bus and we chatted and played.

But now, I'm lying here all by myself. Alone.

I shut my eyes tighter to sleep, but my brain keeps producing images. Images of different scenes from the trip. They're so vivid that the gap between then and now threatens to paralyze me.

It's then that something hits me like a comet. *I wish he were here.* The house feels so empty without him. Too quiet and too lonely. It's as if the two days spent with my friends has reminded me how lonely and boring it is to be at home without my little brother.

Searching for Connection

Something I love doing these days: drawing cartoon pictures of my brother. Along with my idol Sailor Moon, I've started drawing my brother and his toy buses.

Drawing a cartoon picture of my brother isn't too difficult, thanks to his perfectly round face and his very basic hairstyle. First I draw a circle for his face, then carve out a crescent shape from the top of the circle, which I colour in black to represent his bangs. Then I draw his eyes, nose, and mouth ... and there we go, my brother's cute face!

After the first few drafts, I've also added two little lines of hair in the middle of his bangs to express his mischievous personality.

Wherever I find a blank space on a piece of paper, I draw a cartoon of my little brother with his toy buses. My two best friends tell me it really looks like him, and that encourages me to draw more pictures.

One evening, just before supper, I'm watching a TV program. It's the one that comes after my favourite ninja boys anime series, and I normally don't watch it. But today, supper isn't ready yet, and I linger in front of the screen.

In this episode, one of the program hosts visits a small local plush doll shop to make a doll modelled after him with the help of the shop owner. The process doesn't look too complicated, and at the end, he's holding a large plush doll that really looks like him.

As soon as the program is over, I run to my mother in the kitchen. "I want to make a plush doll of my brother!" I exclaim.

For a moment, my mother appears clueless what I'm even talking about. But as I explain more and understanding dawns on her, she hesitates. "A plush doll of your brother?"

She tries to talk me out of the idea, saying it's difficult to make a plush doll, but my mind is already set. "You can help me, Mommy, can't you?"

After a few more unsuccessful attempts to distract me, my mother sighs and agrees to help me make one.

After supper, my mother sets up a small, low table in the living room with a box of sewing tools and pieces of old clothes. She instructs me to draw a picture of my brother on a piece of paper to use as a pattern.

"Just the face? Or the whole body?"

"You want the plush doll of his whole body, don't you?"

When I nod, she tells me to draw the whole body. Because I don't know how we're going to use this picture, I draw not only the outline but also my brother's smiley face and his signature jeans.

My mother pins my drawing to a piece of cloth and cuts the cloth along the pattern. She makes two identical shapes and sews them together.

While we're sewing, my father comes home from work. "Are you two sewing or something?" he asks us from the kitchen, sitting down and helping himself to his dinner on the table. My father's surprise is not unreasonable since it's rare for the sewing box to make an appearance in our household.

"Well, our daughter wants to make a plush doll of her brother," replies my mother, rolling her eyes. "So that's what we're doing!"

My father continues his curious gaze at our endeavour from the kitchen. Once he's done eating, he calls me for the bedtime story. The sewing isn't yet done, but my mother says I can go and she'll complete the rest.

Currently, my father is reading *Jim Button and Luke the Engine Driver* by Michael Ende. We're at the part where a funny creature with one tooth appears and I'm roaring with laughter when my mother comes over with a plush doll in her hand.

"Is it done?" I stop laughing.

"Half-done," my mother replies as she places the doll next to my face. "We'll do the face tomorrow."

The doll has no face or clothes yet, but it has a human shape. A special feeling fills my heart.

After my father finishes reading for the night and leaves the room, I look at the blank plush doll next to my face and feel it with my hand many times before falling asleep.

In early July, preparation for the *Tanabata* festival begins at my kindergarten. My teacher hands out small pieces of colourful paper where we write down our wishes. These pieces of paper will be hung on the little bamboo tree set up in the corner of our front garden so that on July seventh, our wishes will be heard by the stars.

"Write down your wishes," my teacher tells the class. "Your most important wishes – and then we'll hang them on the bamboo tree and wait for your wishes to come true!"

I have many wishes, but when it comes to the most important wishes, there's just one. I want my brother to come back. Nothing would make me happier than to see him again.

But that's not what I write on my *Tanabata* wish paper. Because from what I understand, *Tanabata* is different from magic. It cannot bring a dead person back to life. So I write down my second most important wish. "Please, bring me a little brother or a little sister."

Since my brother passed away, I've been feeling so lonely at home that I want company. I know he or she won't be the same as my brother, but still, we could do many things together – from sharing our snacks to playing together until bedtime.

Day after day, I wait for my mother to tell me we'll be having a new baby in our family. Little do I know that my parents have decided not to have any more children after my brother's death.

One summer day, I find a small notebook among my mother's books and notebooks. It has a blue spine and fits in my hands perfectly.

"Mommy, can I have this?"

"Sure, but what are you going to use it for?" My mother is busy cleaning the house.

"I don't know yet," I answer. "But I like it and I want to keep it!"

I carry the notebook with me, and before long, I have something I want to write about. I crouch on the floor of the back room with a pencil in my hand. I scribble down the title:

"My Brother in the Cradle." I recall the day I met my brother at home for the first time.

My brother was a tiny baby then. I'd just come home from my first long stay at my grandmother's. My mother let me hold him, and whenever he was lying in the cradle alone, I made sure I was by his side, gently rocking the cradle and talking to him.

As I write, it's as if the scene is happening in front of me. A sense of pride fills my heart – the pride for becoming a caring big sister. A smile tugs at my lips.

Once the story is complete, I add a little illustration of me rocking the cradle and my brother lying in it.

The next day, I write another story of my brother with an illustration. And this becomes my habit – every day I sit in a corner of our tiny home and write about my brother in the little notebook. Time stops as I go into each memory of my brother, scribbling words down in my notebook, often giggling and laughing.

The notebook is soon filled with different stories of my brother, and I decide to make it a gift to my mother. The title of the book is *Maiko and Her Little Brother*. I write that on the front cover of the notebook with a black marker, then glue a red bow in the middle to make it look like a gift.

"Mommy, I have something for you." I run to my mother one morning. "Guess what? It's a book!"

As soon as my mother stops the vacuum cleaner, I hand her the little notebook.

"What a surprise!" she exclaims as she takes the notebook in her hands. "Let's have a look!"

The moment she opens the notebook and starts reading, however, my mother becomes quiet. A tight smile appears on her lips and her eyes glisten – the look she always has when remembering my brother.

"Do you like it?" I eagerly ask her.

"This is wonderful, sweetie," she replies, wiping away her tears. "I *love* it."

The notebook finds a home inside the brown cabinet where my mother keeps the family's important items along with plates and cutlery. Whenever we have a guest, my mother takes it out and shares it with them over tea and snacks as she recounts the story of my brother's life and passing. And I see the magic – our guest's face lighting up upon reading my little notebook, sometimes even breaking into laughter.

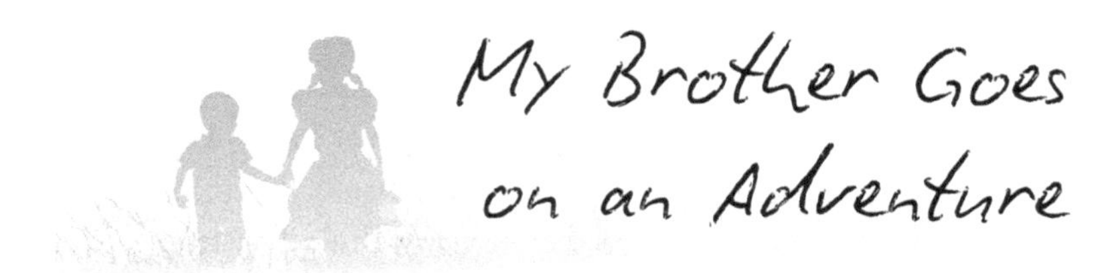

My Brother Goes on an Adventure

Shortly after I finish the little book of memories of my brother, a most exciting idea occurs to me. My brother used to have a collection of toy buses. What if these toy buses were alive? What if they could go on an adventure with my brother?

I pick up a blank notebook and imagine the first scene. My brother is playing with his toy buses in the living room as usual. Suddenly, one of them starts talking, shocking my brother. Just as he tries to run away, his other buses also come to life, chatting loudly.

Grinning, I turn the first page of my notebook and start jotting down the scene.

One day, my brother finds an ad about a hidden treasure. Guess what – the treasure is a box of brand-new toy buses! There is a map attached to this advertisement. He decides to go on an adventure to find this box of treasure.

My brother's original plan is to go on this adventure by himself, but his chatty toy buses won't leave him alone. Calling him their master, they insist on coming with him. Together, their grand adventure begins.

From what I observed in my favourite books like *Winnie the Pooh* and *The Hobbit,* every adventure book should have a map at the beginning. So at the beginning of my book, I include a hand-drawn map of my brother's treasure hunt for the reader.

Once the book is complete, I bring it to my mother, who then brings it to my father, who jokes after reading it that I'm a great writer who cannot write *kanji* (*Chinese characters we learn at school. As a preschooler, I didn't yet know *kanji*, so I wrote everything in *hiragana*).

Since I've had so much fun writing the adventure story, I decide to write a sequel. It's a story of another treasure hunt, but this time with more toy buses because the ones my brother gained in his previous adventure are also coming along with him.

I continue writing sequels, eventually creating a series of six books over the next two years. I invite whoever comes to our home to read them. I find delight in catching those moments when their eyes widen with surprise or their face breaks into laughter as they turn the pages.

The Move

In October, my family moves to a new house in a suburb. My parents didn't choose the condo like the model home we went to see together back in spring. Now that my brother is gone, there's no reason for us to live close to the large hospital. That's how my mother explained it. I guess that makes sense.

My parents are eager about the move, especially my father. It's finally time to move out of this small, rundown place and live in a house where we have a proper bedroom, a dining space separate from the kitchen, and a bathroom free of pill bugs.

But none of these things really excites me.

This is my home. The only home I've lived as long as I can remember. It's not small – think about all the places my friends and I get to explore every day! The square playground. The old Japanese plum tree. The bush on the hilltop next to my brother's favourite bus-watching spot. And many more hidden corners only we children know about.

This community is where I have my best friends, my kindergarten, and all my memories with my brother. I don't want to move. I want to stay right here in my paradise.

But what can I do to change my parents' minds?

Before I know it, the preparation begins. We make multiple trips to the residential development office responsible for our new home. Gifts are bought for my friends, and my new kindergarten is picked. And I carry on with my days.

Some days before our move, my mother takes pictures of every part of our tiny apartment we've called home. In particular, she spends a long time taking many pictures of the wall where my brother's enormous Kind Sun shines.

"Once we paint the wall, it won't be visible anymore," she says, trying different angles with her camera. "Oh, what a *great* drawing..."

I wonder if this is the same mother who scolded us harshly that day when my brother and I had a blast drawing on the wall. She was mad then. But now, there are tears in her eyes as she takes photos, one after another, of my brother's drawing on the wall.

One morning in late October, I go to kindergarten as usual. But as I leave my tiny apartment, I know I won't be returning to this home anymore. Today is the day all the furniture will be sent to our new home. When I finish kindergarten this afternoon, my friend's mother will drive me and my two best friends to my new home. My other friends will also come over, and together, we'll have a house-warming party.

I get so excited thinking about the party that all my other emotions fall by the wayside. I forget that I'm leaving my old home for good and tomorrow won't be the same as today.

My friends and I spend the afternoon playing games in the playground next to my new home until dusk. When we finally come inside, the food is ready. We all sit around the low table reserved for children and help ourselves to the delicious dishes our mothers have prepared. We chat and laugh nonstop while eating, and as soon as the meal is over, we decide to play hide and seek.

One of my friends and I hide inside the tiny washroom upstairs. While hiding there, I notice the interesting pattern on the floor: many tiny dots are printed on the cream background.

"They look like grains of sand, don't they?" I whisper to my friend, following the dotted pattern on the floor with my finger.

"Yeah, they do," my friend replies.

"Maybe we're sitting on the seaside!" My voice rises with excitement. "Can you hear the sound of waves nearby?"

Before we know it, we're playing with the "sand" on the washroom floor, forgetting about hide and seek altogether.

Suddenly, the door is flung open, revealing my friends standing there.

"We're going home now," one of them says to me. "We came to say goodbye."

"Going home?" I repeat blankly. "You're going home?"

From the hallway, I hear adults talking and preparing to leave. They're all going home now.

"Your mom was looking for you," she informs my friend sitting on the washroom floor with me.

Feeling the magic of the evening disappear, I stare at the floor. To my eyes, the dotted pattern still looks like sand.

My friends each say goodbye to me before going downstairs to meet their mothers. Not wanting to be left behind alone with my imagination, I quickly follow them to the hallway.

My mother and I wave at our guests as they get inside their cars and slowly depart to head back home – to the community which used to be *my* home until yesterday.

I wave until the last car turns the corner and its tail lamp disappears into darkness. I then dash inside the house to find all the traces of our fun time and say my own goodbye to each of them.

Only Child

One day, I'm walking down the street with my mother when we bump into the mother of someone we know. She and my mother start chatting, and after a while, I hear a question. "Do you have any siblings?"

I almost sigh because I know how this conversation is going to go.

"Well ..." I open my mouth, and my mother cuts in.

"I had a son younger than her, but we lost him."

"Oh, I'm so sorry." The lady's kind face fills with sympathy. I look at her face very carefully to see if she's just saying it, or she actually means it. Her expression looks genuine. A tiny hope takes root as the lady opens her mouth again. "So, you're an only child now."

My disappointment is huge. All the more so because I thought maybe she'd say something different and ask more about my brother. But instead, she said what many others before her had said: an *only child*.

My mother has just told her I had a brother. If she really heard that, she wouldn't call me an only child because having a sibling once means having one forever. You don't stop having a brother just because he's physically gone.

I want to tell all of this to the lady, but I know she's kind and means well. So I keep my mouth shut and don't say anything.

Missing You Still

Spring of 1998. I've just turned eight. One day, I find an old blank notebook among my mother's work documents. These days, I've been thinking how if my brother were alive, he'd be starting kindergarten this month. As I flip through the blank notebook, his first day at kindergarten plays in my mind.

In this daydream, we still live in that tiny old apartment, and my brother is going to the same kindergarten I did.

Early in the morning of his first day as a kindergartener, my brother's cheerful voice echoes in the living room. Too excited, he woke up a few hours earlier than usual, and is now checking his bag contents one by one. Once he goes through all the items, he starts all over again. Eventually, his loud voice wakes up our mother. When she hands him his lunch box, my brother heads out to kindergarten on his own, singing a song he's just made up to express how happy he is on this special day.

In the story, I also make an appearance, and we interact just like any other siblings in the world. The time I spend writing is when I live in this alternative reality where that community of apartments is still our home and nothing is lacking from my life, with all my family and friends right beside me.

My new house has a garden. The first spring after we moved, my father planted several flowers, and among them was a pot of hydrangeas. Now it has grown into a proper bush, and every June, right as the rainy season arrives, its flowers bloom in deep blue: the same colour as the ones we saw at the hospital parking lot years ago when my brother was a newborn staying in the ICU.

Around my brother's birthday, my mother cuts one hydrangea bloom from the bush, puts it in a vase and places it on my brother's altar. Even when all other plants in the garden suffer from malnutrition and diseases, the blue hydrangeas thrive on. We call them my brother's hydrangeas.

In May, my father's university friend visits our home and gives me a copy of the book *The Robber Hotzenplotz* by Otfried Preussler. It's an adventure story of two little boys in rural Germany who fights off the robber Hotzenplotz and his friend and evil wizard using their smart brains and brave hearts.

Near the climax of the story, the bad wizard becomes upset with Hotzenplotz and uses a charm to summon him. All he needs is an item that belongs to Hotzenplotz. Drawing a circle around Hotzenplotz's hat, the wizard chants a spell, and in a matter of seconds, Hotzenplotz appears at the centre of the circle.

I'm reading the book alone in my darkened room. The sun has set, but I've been too absorbed in the story to even notice it. Now, my face glows with enthusiasm.

This is it! I look up. *I can use this.*

I run downstairs and march into the kitchen where my mother is preparing supper.

"Mommy, can I use one of my brother's buses?" I point at my brother's toy bus collection placed on his altar in the living room.

"What is it for?"

"I've just discovered a spell that can summon a missing person," I reply breathlessly. "So, I'll be summoning my brother using his bus!"

There's a brief pause before she replies, "Okay."

Picking up one of my brother's toy buses, I also remember to ask my mother for permission to do some drawing on the floor.

"I need to draw something on the floor for this magic to work. But don't worry," I quickly add. "I'll use a pencil, and I'll erase it after I try the spell!"

With that, I run back upstairs to my room.

I follow the instruction in the book carefully. I place the toy bus on the floor and draw a circle, then chant the spell like the wizard did in the book.

Nothing happens.

I try again.

Still, nobody appears. All my excitement evaporates.

A few minutes later, I walk into the living room with my head down.

"So, how did it go?" asks my mother as I approach my brother's altar.

"It didn't work."

"I see." My mother doesn't say anything further.

I put back the toy bus with my brother's collection, then return to my room to erase the circle on the floor.

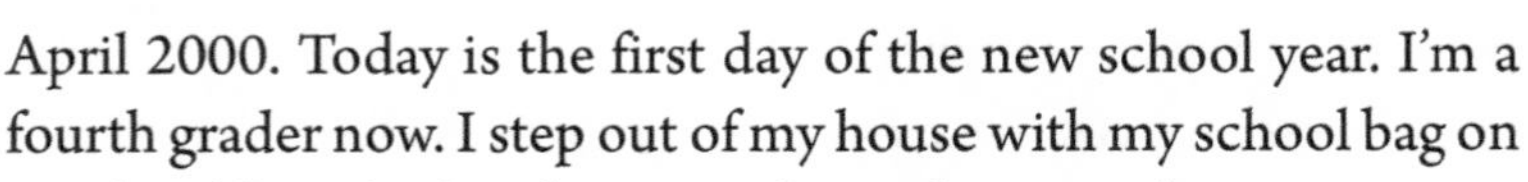

April 2000. Today is the first day of the new school year. I'm a fourth grader now. I step out of my house with my school bag on my shoulder. It's a bright sunny day with a warm breeze.

A sense of excitement fills my heart as I march through the playground behind my house. Everything feels fresh. My classmates remain the same as last year, but we'll have a new teacher. Who will it be? And what about my new seat? Who will I be sitting next to?

Just when I come out of the playground onto a wide street, I spot a familiar figure ahead of me. It's my friend. I'm about to run up to her when I notice another smaller figure walking beside her, holding my friend's hand. There's a bright yellow cover on her brand-new schoolbag, signaling that she's a first grader. Today is the first school day for my friend's little sister.

Not far from them, I spot another girl walking with her little sister whose schoolbag also has the yellow cover.

Suddenly, my step slows down. Eyes trained on the two little girls walking next to my friends, I swallow a lump in my throat.

He should've been here, a voice rings in my head. *My brother is also starting school today.*

A tingly sensation fills my nose, followed by dampness in my eyes. I quickly look up to push back my tears, even though nobody is watching.

I remain still until my throat isn't too tight anymore. When both my friends have gone far down the street, I finally start moving. But I dare not make a sound. I tiptoe behind them so my presence won't be discovered.

Later that day, I sit in front of a piece of paper, this morning's incident replaying in my mind over and over. One thought keeps coming back.

Nobody saw my brother this morning except me. Why?

Because he died. Not yesterday, but four years ago. To people's eyes, I'm an only child. My brother's passing is a story of the past that happened a long time ago.

But it's not.

My brother's passing is not a story of the past.

Otherwise, how could I have felt what I felt this morning? The stinging pain was as if I stumbled on a whole new abyss inside my heart. This one is different from the hole I felt right after his passing. This one is new.

I jot down words as they explode in my head. I'm addressing the people who fail to see what I can see and feel. What's visible physically isn't everything that exists in this world. There are things that can only be seen with our hearts, and those are as real as the person in front of us, or the road that we walk on.

The words eventually form a poem. A poem that describes the day as my heart has seen it. I'm walking to school with my brother, hand in hand, congratulating him on his first day at school and feeling ever prouder as his big sister.

Winter 2000, in arts and crafts class. We're starting our paper print project today. With a large blank sheet of paper in front of me, I'm listening to my teacher explain the procedure to the class when a brilliant design idea comes to me.

My brother rides on his ride-on car. But this one's shaped like a bus!

A smile tugs at my lips. The image is crystal clear in my mind.

As soon as my teacher finishes the instructions, I pick up a pen to draw the design on the paper. While my classmates are busy chatting around me, I become absorbed in the happy world where my brother is riding a bus-shaped ride-on car. With one arm raised, he's shouting something. Yes, I can hear him. He's saying, "Let's go!"

"What are you drawing?" somebody asks me from across the table.

"This is my brother," I reply without looking up. "He's riding a bus-shaped ride-on car. My brother loves buses!"

I talk about my brother so often that everybody in my class knows I once had a little brother who was a great bus-lover. The only difference at the moment is that I talk about him in present tense. When I'm immersed in my creative world, time stops existing, and my brother becomes as present as anybody else in the room.

Once the design is complete, I choose bright yellow as the background colour so that it looks like my brother is riding his bus in the sunlight. My teacher helps me with the printing process on the final day of the project.

"It's turned out great," he says as he hands me my printed picture. "Your brother's looking very cute."

I'm too busy checking the outcome of my paper print to reply, but my smile grows bigger upon hearing my teacher's words, especially the part where he said my brother looks cute.

Special Giveaway

Download a copy of *My Little Brother Picture Book,* a collection of photos and accompanying stories of me and my brother.

Afterword

In May 2022, I was sitting at a table inside the Ottawa office of the Bereaved Families of Ontario (BFO) with seven other women and two facilitators during an eight-week group grief therapy program. We each had lost someone significant in our lives and were there for the opportunity to heal together.

More than twenty-five years had passed since my brother's passing, and I'd never done any grief therapy regarding my loss until then. The thought hadn't even occurred to me because it had been a long time since his departure, and I believed I'd made peace with it.

But that spring, as I started thinking about having my own family, I was suddenly swallowed by an immense sadness that took me back to the memories of my brother. That's when I realized there might still be some unexplored grief around his passing. I signed up for the BFO's group therapy session.

Every Wednesday evening, the ten of us would meet for two hours and work on a themed art project to connect with the person we each lost and wanted to honour. At the end of each session, we went around the table, explaining the meaning of our artwork and talking about a memory of the person.

When it was my turn, I found myself talking enthusiastically about my brother as if he were there. Someone pointed out how my face lit up as I spoke about him. I'd never talked about my brother in such detail in the presence of others, and the experience of sharing enlivened a part of me that was long buried.

In the summer of 2022, I started working on the manuscript of *My Little Brother*. Before that, I'd been writing selected memories of my brother on my blog, but my decision to make them into a book allowed me to revisit all the memories of my early life with my brother more closely and thoroughly.

As I wrote about the day when I learned of my brother's death, the pain of loss was still as raw as what I felt that day. I'd still break into sobs just as I did in my mother's lap that morning. And I still regretted not seeing off my brother on the day of his heart operation just as I did back then.

Even now, after so many years since his passing, when people ask me if I have siblings, I tell them I once had a brother three years younger than me. The two years and nine months my brother spent on this planet have left a permanent mark on my life. They taught me the joy of being a big sister, and his absence taught me the value of life and of things that cannot be seen with our eyes.

This book is my brother's and my joint project. It is our hope that the book serves as an invitation for each of us to fully treasure the gifts left by our loved ones and to start sharing them with those who are around us today.

Acknowledgements

I am forever grateful to all the people who made my early childhood what it is – a happy place I can always come back to whenever I feel lost in my adult life. I want to express my special thanks to: my mother and father, who not only kept a roof over my brother's and my heads but also gifted us with fun days in a shabby home filled with adventures; my late maternal grandmother, who was always by my side whenever my parents were busy with my brother and made sure I felt loved; my kindergarten teachers, who treated all of us, including our little siblings, with enormous love; people inside the community of tiny, half-dilapidated apartments, whose presence made each day an unforgettable adventure; and my two best friends, Sakura and Karen, and their families, who really knew my brother and who always made me feel seen and understood whenever I needed support in my grief journey after my brother's passing.

I want to express my deep gratitude to the Bereaved Families of Ontario and the women I met inside the group grief therapy session. It was a profound experience for me to have the opportunity to really talk about the memories of my brother in the presence of others, and to listen to others talk about the memories of their loved ones. Without those eight weeks, I may not have decided to write this book.

I would like to thank my two brilliant editors, D'Ann Mateer and Elisabeth Adams, for working with me on this project with such profound care. Their insights and edits allowed this story to fully come to life while ensuring a smooth reading experience.

The writing and publishing process of this book was supported by the Self-Publishing School community. I am especially grateful to my coaches, Andrew Biernat, Brittany Plumeri, and Barbara Hartzler for holding me accountable throughout this journey.

Finally, but not least importantly, I express my special thanks to my reader. You are the reason why I have written this book. Thank you for allowing me the joy of sharing this story with you.

Stay in Touch

Thank you so much for reading the book to the end!

To personally stay in touch with me and join my future book journey, follow the link below to become part of Maiko's Letter Community! In addition to my book updates, you'll get a Story Letter from me every Saturday in your inbox – a mini story from my real life that's going to light up your day with love.

Link: subscribepage.io/mylittlebrother

Much love and appreciation,

Maiko

About the Author

Maiko Serizawa is a storyteller and mathematician living in Ottawa. What inspired her onto the journey of story writing was the early loss of her younger brother at the age of six. At the time, she wrote a series of adventure stories starring her brother and discovered the healing power in writing. As a writer, her mission is to tap into our heart's forgotten treasures through subtle stories found in our day-to-day life. She loves visiting coffee shops for writing, and her debut novel *Olive's Diary* was inspired by her favourite café in Ottawa and her years of experience at different coffee shops around the world.

You can connect with her on her website https://www.maple-and-olive.com/. She is also a host of the weekly show *Maiko's Story Photograph Podcast* available on Spotify and Apple Podcasts.